WHAT PEOPLE ARE SAYING ABOUT
INTENTIONAL LEADERSHIP . . .

Intentional Leadership makes the complex discernible and, more importantly, useable. I found a hunger in turning the pages. Enjoy the reading; I did.

—Lorn H. Adkins, LCP, LMFT, National Board for Certified Counselors member

Intentional Leadership gives you a blueprint for life and a plan to help you identify and reach those goals that sound oh-so-simple but tend to be oh-so-difficult to attain.

—Jerry Brewton, speaker, author, President of Brewton Insurance, Inc.

Intentional Leadership identifies those crucial elements a leader must focus on to create the future and navigate the hurdles that inevitably appear along the way.

—Robert Hopper, Senior Vice President, RSI Church Solutions

Intentional Leadership is relevant for corporate leaders as well as all individuals who want to live their life with more intention and purpose.

—Susan Vitalis, MD, author of *Still Listening: How to Hear God's Direction at Life's Crossroads*

Intentional Leadership shows us that sometimes asking the right questions is the most powerful tool for getting where we want to go. It doesn't have to be complicated, it just has to be intentional.

**—Amy Hoppock, professional coach, Aloha Consulting,
author of *32 Questions: A Personal Quest through Questions
for Parents, Professionals, and Business Teams***

Intentional Leadership takes you on a virtual voyage toward your best self and best results. For any person or leader who is ready to elevate their life or company to new heights, this book will provide a smooth navigation system.

**—Laetitia Mizero Hellerud, founder and owner of Ubuntu
Consulting, social justice activist, inclusion advocate, author**

Dave Weitz leads with humility, passion, and experience. Before I got even one chapter into *Intentional Leadership*, he had challenged me to act and determine my destination.

**—Erin Foley, author of *Kapuna:
How Love Transformed a Culture***

Intentional Leadership provides a valuable contribution to anyone interested in expanding their leadership capacity. You'll find this book an engaging, practical, and solid resource in the development of intentional leadership.

**—Dan Copp, Church of the Nazarene, Education Commissioner
for the International Board of Education**

I would read anything written by Dave Weitz, including scrawls on a napkin; he's that caliber of thinker and leader. I'm confident that *Intentional Leadership* will help leaders reach for and grasp personal and professional leadership goals. Read on!

—Ron Wilbur, President, Luminor Strategic Communications

Intentional Leadership weaves incredible, compelling truths throughout the book. This work will captivate and motivate people from all walks of life to reach their true potential.

—Lisa Harper, founder of Marathon Mission, nineteen-time marathoner, author of *Living and Loving—The Marathon of Life*

As a professional life coach for nearly twenty years, I have learned that the only people who arrive at their dreams are the ones who clearly articulate their destination. *Intentional Leadership* will take every reader on a journey toward clarifying their vision, while honoring the personal heart behind the journey.

—Kim Fletcher, life coach, speaker, and author of *Unlikely Mentors*

INTENTIONAL LEADERSHIP

HOW THE BEST LEADERS CREATE THE FUTURE

DAVE WEITZ

Foreword by Mike McHargue

Intentional Leadership: How the Best Leaders Create the Future
Dave Weitz © 2017

Print ISBN: 978-1-61206-131-3
eBook ISBN: 978-1-61206-132-0

Cover Design credit to Adam Weitz/The New Harbor Company, NewHarborCo.com
Interior and Cover Design by: Fusion Creative Works, FusionCW.com
Lead Editor: Jennifer Regner

For more information, visit IntentionialLeadershiptheBook.com

Published by

ALOHA
PUBLISHING

AlohaPublishing.com

First Printing
Printed in the United States of America

For Kathy–

Your influence is in everything I do.

CONTENTS

FOREWORD

I love clarity.

I work with executive teams to help them clearly see what they are good at (and not good at!) behaviorally and develop a clear plan for how they will improve. Likewise, I help executive leaders achieve intellectual clarity by helping them answer important questions like "How do we behave?" and "What is most important, right now?" based upon Patrick Lencioni's Table Group methodologies.

Intentional Leadership **offers clarity for those who want to be a good leader, both in their organization and in their life, but need a clear path to do so.**

I love simplicity.

My library of business books includes many that are long, complex, and unread past the third or fourth chapter. Simplicity in a book or a plan is more difficult to create than complexity or confusion in one is. The rewards of simplicity are great. Simple messages and simple plans can be readily received and applied by a much larger population and therefore have far greater impact.

Intentional Leadership **tells it like it is. Without excess or redundancy, this no-nonsense offering gets to the heart of what it takes to be a good leader.**

I love a good, thoughtful plan.

Yogi Berra famously once said, "If you don't know where you're going, you'll end up someplace else." This sounds obvious and silly, to be sure, but the underlying points—that direction and a plan are important—are undoubtedly true, and they are especially true for a leader. An organization or a team without a clear plan will not find success. Success doesn't happen by accident.

Intentional Leadership **offers a thoughtful plan that is sure to put you on a path to success. By asking the right questions, Dave Weitz challenges you to determine a well-thought-out plan to where it is you actually want to go.**

Because I love clarity, simplicity, and a thoughtful plan, I love *Intentional Leadership*. If you apply these concepts with the teams you lead or in your personal life, I'm confident you will achieve the success you seek—as an influencer, leader, or manager of any endeavor.

Mike McHargue
President, M5 Partners
Principal Consultant, Table Group Consulting

INTRODUCTION

JUST BECAUSE IT'S SIMPLE DOESN'T MEAN IT'S EASY

I sat on a Sunday evening with a client in a Starbucks not far up the street from my home. Since she was also a dear friend, I had no problem taking time out from a weekend to talk about the future of her company.

She was seeking to transition her company. She wasn't sure exactly which direction she wanted to go, so we discussed some of the obvious options concerning the future of her organization and her life. We talked about selling off part of the company—that might be a prudent choice. We discussed specializing more and limiting the types of clients she would choose to work with in the days ahead. We even discussed doing nothing.

However, the option to do nothing didn't sit quite true with either of us. We talked about different combinations of these as well as other possibilities.

Then I said, "What you need to do is ask yourself four questions." This is what I had done with my own companies.

She flipped over the page on her pad and grabbed a pen, as if to say, "Okay, I'm ready."

"The first question is, 'Where do I want to go?' In other words, when this is all done, where do you hope to end up? What's your ultimate goal?"

She wrote it down.

"Second," I continued, "'Why do I want to go there?' You need to understand that at the start, because you will need to remind yourself of your *why* throughout the process, especially during the difficult times."

She nodded her head as she wrote it down.

"Next," I said, "you're going to need a plan. So ask yourself, 'How will I get there?' You won't get there by accident, so you'd better put together a plan."

"And, finally," I said as she finished writing the previous question, "ask yourself, 'How will I know when I get there?'"

As she finished writing the last question, she said, "You need to write a book about this."

Hmm. I had used those questions many times in the past. This was the first time someone had responded with, "You should write a book."

I don't remember what I said, but I remember thinking, "Yeah—easier said than done."

But—here we are.

And, it *was* easier said than done. Most things are.

In fact, many simple things aren't easy to do.

For example, it's not complicated to get your finances in order and get out of debt. Simply spend less than you earn. Quit using your credit cards so much. Pay yourself first and put money in a savings account for emergencies or a rainy day. Put together a spending plan (a better choice of words than "budget") and then live by it.

As Will Rogers said, "Too many people spend money they haven't earned on things they don't want, to impress people they don't like." See? Simple. But that doesn't mean it's easy to do.

Or how about losing weight? Eat less and exercise more. Count the calories you put into your system. Pay attention to the types of food you eat. Stop eating so much sugar. Quit eating processed foods and eat more natural food products. Cut out the fast food and the trans fats—skip the fries and the chips and eat more salads.

And, by the way, you don't need to stop at a coffee shop every morning for that oversized white chocolate mocha to get your day started. Or the chocolate chip and cream dessert drink on the way home.

Exercise? It's simple: put your running shoes on, walk out the front door, and keep putting one foot in front of the other. Lifting weights is just as simple. Pick up weight, lift it, put it down. It can't get much less complicated than that.

Aren't you glad you bought this book? Already, in the first couple of pages, we've helped you lose weight and get your finances in order. It's that simple—and you're welcome.

But here's the thing. Seventy-six percent of Americans live paycheck to paycheck. More than two-thirds of Americans are overweight. Simple doesn't mean easy to achieve. If simple meant easy, then we'd all be millionaires and at a perfect, healthy weight.[1]

So . . . please, *please* do not confuse my message. It's not easy—but it will definitely be worth it. I have learned in more than a quarter century in leadership that while not that complicated, leading anything is incredibly hard.

This book is about four simple questions you can use to build a clear and compelling picture of where you're going and why—in a relatively short period of time. In reality, it's a process. And, with a little more time invested, you can figure out how to get there. It's a simple process—it doesn't require a "blue-ribbon panel," a months-long study, or hundreds of wasted man-hours.

Come along with me to learn from the stories I've shared and work through the outlined steps—and you'll not only possess a clear picture of your goal and the path to get there, you'll know how to communicate it in a compelling way.

Communicate your vision so that it grips your heart, captivates the people you work with, and drives your organization or life forward with power.

Once you do this, you'll be able to move confidently in the direction you are sure is the right one. And the people for whom you are responsible, be it your company, your division, your department, or your family, will gladly and confidently go with you.

Spend some time with the four simple questions that follow. Share them with some of your key people—and if, together, you take the time to honestly and clearly answer them, the result of the process could be an amazing journey. A journey of success, accomplishment, and fulfillment beyond your previous experience.

The beauty of this simple exercise lies in the fact that it has universal application, no matter the situation. It's like climbing a tall tree and scanning the horizon. And it will ensure you are intentionally going in the right direction.

Maybe you're in the middle of a midlife or midcourse correction. You've discovered you need to go in a totally different direction. But where? "Which direction should I choose? Is this the right one? If it is, how will I get there?"

Wherever you are at this moment, whether you're leading a company, an organization, or your own life, make the decision to *intentionally* lead. You can be confident that you're heading in the right direction, motivated by the right reasons, and with a plan that is guaranteed to get you there.

As you journey through the pages ahead, you'll unpack and examine the four simple questions I asked my friend that Sunday evening. These are the same questions I've asked about my own life, and posed to others.

Where do you want to go?

Why do you want to go there?

How will you get there?

How will you know when you get there?

A little explanation will help you understand the process. "Where do you want to go?" deals with direction, or as I have used it here, destination. It's the vision question. Sometimes the journey *is* the destination, which redefines the destination as a direction. What do you see your company trying to accomplish? What are the goals you want to achieve in your own life? Where do you see yourself, or your organization, being three, five, ten years from now? Where do you want to go in life? What do you want to accomplish?

The second incredibly important question asks, "Why do you want to go there?" Why do you think those objectives are the ones for you and/or the organization you're leading? Why are these more important than others? Why did this direction jump out at you more than any other? If you haven't thought about these *why* questions, multiple other possibilities or obstacles, and even people, can too easily dissuade you from your chosen path.

"How will I get there?" This is really, what's your plan? What are the strategic steps, the tactics, the tools I need? Who do I need on my team? If your destination or goal is important, develop a practical plan to get there.

"How will I know when I get there?" clarifies the results. What will it look like? What will you see? The concept here is to clarify a complete "picture" of what you're trying to accomplish. If you're trying to increase revenue, your CFO's financial reports will reflect that. If you're trying to build a new manufacturing complex, your company will have moved in and started producing your product from the new facility. If you want to increase your web traffic, the numbers will indicate that. You will know when you get to your destination because you know what you're looking for.

Start by asking yourself these simple questions. I guarantee they will lead you to the right destination and you can experience the joy and fulfillment that floods your being when you get to where you want to go.

1

WHAT'S THE DESTINATION?

"Would you tell me, please,
which way I ought to go from here?"

"That depends a good deal on where you
want to get to," said the Cat.

"I don't much care where–" said Alice.

"Then it doesn't matter which way you go,"
said the Cat.

—Lewis Carroll, *Alice's Adventures in Wonderland*

On a sunny day, my lifelong hero stands poised in his back-
yard ready to begin target practice in the hopes of perfecting his
archery skills. He pulls an arrow from the quiver, positioning
it for the perfect shot. He draws back on the string and sights
down the shaft of the arrow to make sure it will land precisely
where he hopes.

He lets go of the string, propelling the arrow through the air and into the fence with a decisive thud. Then Charlie Brown runs over to the fence, pulls a piece of chalk out of his pocket, and draws a bull's-eye around where the arrow landed. And then he draws another circle around the bull's-eye, and another and another to complete the target.

He trots back to his starting position, pulls another arrow out of his quiver and repeats the process—positions the arrow, draws back the string, sights down the arrow, and releases the string, propelling the arrow toward the fence. Again, he runs over to the fence and draws the bull's-eye and successive circles around where the arrow has landed in his fence.

As usual, Lucy stands nearby, watching the whole ordeal unfold. With her typical smug and condescending tone, she scolds my hero.

"Charlie Brown, you blockhead. That is *not* how you do target practice!"

"Yes," Charlie Brown responds, "but if you do it my way, you never miss."

I've told that story in speeches and talks for several years. It never fails to draw a positive response from the crowd—a guaranteed chuckle.

In all honesty, it's not as amusing to me as it used to be. It's still funny and still makes the point, but it's become more of a metaphor rather than a humorous anecdote.

The more coaching and consulting I do, the more the story has grown to represent the way many leaders run their organizations, and how an even larger number of people live their lives. No clear direction, no specific destination. They let the arrow of their life fly and where it lands, that's where they draw the bull's-eye.

If you lived a solitary life on a deserted island, that philosophy would prove sufficient. But if you're leading an organization, it falls massively short. People depend on you for leadership—their livelihood and that of their families depend not only on how well they do their job but on how well you lead them and their fellow workers. The success of the company depends on a clear direction and purpose.

What's true for organizations is also true for an individual. You need clear direction. I recently listened to an interview with a businessman who, over the course of his life, has built eight different businesses and sold several of them to Fortune 500 companies. He never *has* to work again. In fact, he's retired three times—and each time he's retired, he has gained 50 pounds. And each time, his wife woke him up from one of his midday naps and declared, "Look at what's happened to you. You've *got* to find something to do."

And he admits she's right. He has finally concluded, "You can only play so much golf and go fishing so many times." So, three different times, he's found something new to do (and lost the 50 pounds). Today, he runs a successful mentoring and coaching organization that helps thousands of executives successfully navigate the minefields of corporate life.

What I'm suggesting is this: Whether you lead an organization or your own life, one of the most important questions you can ask is, "Where are we going?" or, "Where am I going?"

WHY DESTINATION IS SO IMPORTANT

I grew up as one of those "Can I?" kids. I could be anywhere outside playing, but I had a type of sixth sense that immediately knew when my dad was leaving the house. And whenever he got in the car, whether it was to go pick up the mail at the post office or run to the bank or complete a list of errands, I was in the front seat of the car waiting for him.

"Can I go with you Dad? Can I?" I didn't care if he was taking a load of trash to the landfill, I just wanted to go. I loved going places. I didn't know it as a ten-year-old, but I was captivated by going somewhere. Even at that age, I was "direction-driven."

It wasn't until I got older that I began to care about where I was going—*where*, the destination, became much more important.

People Are Looking for Direction

People are open to being led, and in most companies, expect to be led and will follow—if the leader knows where they are going. Time and again, I have witnessed a leader paint a clear picture of where the organization was going and why it was going there. They had a clear plan for how they would get there and communicated everything in a compelling way. And each time, people followed and, together with the organization, experienced success and growth, and the organization was dominated by a sense of well-being and an incredible level of morale.

People are open to leadership and will follow if they are led responsibly and in a way that invites collaboration.

Direction Helps Avoid Despair and Frustration

A functional definition of despair is getting up day after day after day, doing the same thing, knowing that nothing will ever change. It's depressing to think of a life spent that way.

Something happens to us when we have purpose, when we have direction. And it's pretty powerful.

Famed Starbucks CEO Howard Schultz said, "When you're surrounded by people who share a passionate commitment around a common purpose, anything is possible."

It's a thing of beauty to watch that process in operation, whether it's in a company setting new growth records or while coaching a young entrepreneur who has grabbed hold of a vision that depicts exactly what he wants to accomplish with his life.

As author of *The Light in the Heart*, Roy T. Bennett has said, "If you have a strong purpose in life, you don't have to be pushed. Your passion will drive you there."

Further, it doesn't matter what arises or what stands in the way. A person or organization with a clear direction is unstoppable.

He who has a why to live for can bear almost any how.

–Friedrich Nietzsche

But something else happens when you don't have purpose, when you set sail, rudderless, with no clear sense of direction. That's why being destination-driven is so important.

In his monumental work, *Deep Change*, Robert E. Quinn[2] addresses what happens when those in leadership ignore the need for appropriate change and instead accept the status quo. In other words, when leaders fail to rise to the challenge, paint a compelling vision of what needs to happen or choose a definite and intentional organizational direction.

"People know when a critical issue is being ignored . . ." Quinn writes. "People slowly lose hope and begin to feel trapped by their circumstances. They often cope by withdrawing, or, conversely, by staying busy with insignificant issues."

The point that cannot be lost in this discussion is this:

"Experience suggests that they would love to consider constructive alternatives, and even at the darkest moment would do so, if given a reason. During troubled times, people thirst for effective leadership. They crave a vision that has credibility."

In Quinn's mind, as noted above, without effective leadership—including communicating a clear and compelling vision (direction)—your organization is either moving forward to embrace deep change or it is dying a slow but certain death.

HOW TO DETERMINE YOUR DESTINATION

The questions you ask to help you determine your direction will be different, depending on whether you are trying to determine the direction of your own life or that of an organization.

You need to ask "What now?" for an individual, and "What's next?" for an organization.

Let me illustrate from a couple of personal experiences.

What Now?

A few months after my 50th birthday, I found myself in a position I hadn't anticipated. My position with the organization I had been leading had come to a close, and so my first inclination was to ask the normal question, "What's next?" Over the next several months, I would learn that I was asking the wrong question.

"What's next?" is the question you ask when you figure you're going to do the same thing you've been doing, only in a different location or with a different organization.

True to form, those opportunities presented themselves. Over the next couple of months, there were offers—all in different locations, and each with its own merit. My wife and I looked at each one, seriously giving them consideration. But none of them seemed "right." Going here would mean this. If I took that position, we would have to do that. Moving there would mean . . .

You know what I mean. You've gone through it, too.

Over time I felt a growing awareness that maybe "What's next?" wasn't the question I needed to be asking. Maybe there was something else for me to do. I didn't know what that was, but the desire to find out was growing.

After multiple evenings spent discussing the options at our favorite restaurant, my wife said, "Let's go for it." And so I made the decision to leave my career of choice of the last 25 years. For what? I hadn't a clue. But that decision changed the question I was asking. I went from asking "What's next?" to asking "What now?"

What am I going to do now? What do I *want* to do now? And . . . wait for it . . . where am I going? All the questions I was asking revolved around direction. Where was I going to go? Not in terms of location, for we had already made the decision to stay in the city where we had lived for the previous ten years. But where was I going, in terms of career? Purpose? Destination? Yes, deciding what I was going to do was important, but that would only be determined by my ultimate destination.

I love and feel compelled to coach individuals who are in that exact stage of life, or who are going through the same type of circumstances. At midlife, they are making a change. They've decided to take a chance. They're asking the question, "What now?" It's a fun and exciting—albeit sometimes scary—time.

"What now?" is the question you need to ask, as an individual, as you determine a new direction.

The question of destination is also crucial when working with an organization. If you are trying to provide a fresh vision for your company, the question to ask is "What's next?"

What's Next?

As an example, I became the leader of an organization that, about three years after I started, was asking, "What's next?"

We had set an aggressive agenda for growth and while our plans were in motion and on schedule, it was time for us to look ahead even farther to set the agenda for the next several years. The senior leadership team and board of directors came together for several extended meeting sessions to set the course for the next chapter of our existence. We were meeting to decide where we were going next.

The agenda was simple; it consisted of a single question: "What's next?" Our discussion revolved around these variations: What were we going to do next? Where were we going to go next? What was our new destination?

We needed to know so we could chart our course, prepare our teams, arrange our resources, and figure out the necessary budget. A key part of this discussion was having the right people in the room.

Make sure you've identified the stakeholders and include them in the process of determining direction. For our company, it was senior leadership and, because of our organization's bylaws, the board of directors. But there were others, too. They were not senior leadership or elected officials, but they were there because they were "influencers." Because we knew the influence they had and the weight they carried, they got a seat at the table. We knew they would play a vital role in communicating to the rest of the organization the decisions we made. They would ensure a positive impact. These people would be cheerleaders; they would help us successfully get where we wanted to go.

When I was asking, "What now?" for my personal life, my wife and I were the key stakeholders. Eventually, as we were contemplating some definite possibilities, I brought my adult son into the discussion. That seemed appropriate, as he likely would be affected by whatever plans we made. And because this was such a monumental shift and change in my life, I sat down separately with some trusted friends and associates. I selected trusted people of depth and integrity to give me feedback and wisdom.

It took a long time with several experiments before I got to where I am today, but the process was dominated by the question of "What now?" to figure out, "Where am I going?"

WHY YOU NEED TO COMMUNICATE THE DESTINATION

Inevitably, in any discussion about destination or vision, the question of *how* or *if* it should be communicated comes up. People ask questions like, "How do I communicate the destination?" and "What if people don't like the destination?" However, these often come after the initial question, "Do I communicate the destination?"

While it may seem like an absurd question ("Of course you communicate the destination," you're thinking), it's really not. If someone has previously attempted to communicate their vision and it did not go well, they will often question this step. Maybe they struggled to communicate it in just the right way. Maybe people resisted, even rebelled. Or misunderstandings blew up— what people heard was not what the leader communicated.

A friend of mine, an extremely successful leader, once led a major directional change in his organization. He did everything right. He had the right people in the room; the move, on the surface, had enjoyed consensus. Everything seemed like it was a "go."

However, when he communicated the destination to the rest of the organization, something went sideways. The decision was not met with acceptance; there were no cheers, only jeers. My friend had been leading his organization for more than fifteen years. He was loved and respected. But even with that history, a mutiny seemed on the horizon, as this new direction was clearly not met with acceptance.

He said of the experience, "I don't think it could have gone worse."

If you have one of those experiences in your past, you may be understandably reluctant to go through that again.

Part of the job description of a leader includes communication. Do not shirk that responsibility—the success and health of your company depends on it. When everyone knows the destination and feels they are a stakeholder, everyone pulls in the same direction. Revenue increases, customer satisfaction rises, worker morale goes up, company growth increases. Why? Because everyone in the company understands where they are going and why.

Let me take it one step farther. If you lead your organization with a clear voice and ask your team for input on how to execute the challenges ahead, they will be far more likely to be on board with your efforts. They cannot help or even do their jobs adequately if they don't know.

Several years ago, I attended a conference in Chicago and toured a large organization known for its amazing growth over the years as well as its excellence and innovation.

It was an impressive place. For a growth junkie like me, it was quite a thrill to hear about their success, their new initiatives, and where they were going next. But what impressed me most was something I'm not sure others on the casual tour noticed.

I knew the company well; I had studied it. I had heard their CEO speak several times and I was well acquainted with his vision and passion for what they were doing. But here's what impressed me: The woman who served as our tour guide that day was just as excited and passionate about what her organization was doing as he was. She was articulating the same vision I had heard from the CEO on several occasions.

The direction of this organization had been communicated so often, so well, and so memorably that our tour guide could share it naturally and succinctly. She was not a company vice president, a division head, or a department chairperson; she was a tour guide—that is to say, she was not among the upper levels of management. In fact, she had volunteered to give the tour.

I discovered that day that one of the secrets to company excellence and effectiveness is for every person at every level to know the answer to the question, "Where are we going?"

This concept also applies to the other three questions we noted earlier. You likewise must share these answers and strategically remind yourself and your people of these answers so they become a natural and organic part of your culture.

HOW TO COMMUNICATE THE DESTINATION

How do you share the destination—the vision, the direction, the *where*—with your people? Here are four simple suggestions.

1. Communicate It Personally and Informally

One of my favorite sources of information on this is an older book: *In Search of Excellence* by Tom Peters and Robert Waterman, Jr.[3] They popularized the phrase "management by walking around," or MBWA. They suggested that one of the best ways to lead your people was to get out of your office every day, or even multiple times each day, simply to wander around the company.

The point was that it is in the break rooms, in the cafeteria, at the coffee station, or maybe when you stop by someone's desk, that you can most effectively connect with your employees. The impact of informal communication—one-on-one or in small groups—is monumental.

At Hewlett-Packard (HP) in Palo Alto, California, it was called "management by *wandering* around." Peters and Waterman pointed out that all of what HP called its "golden rules" involved communicating more. They wrote:

> Even the social and physical settings at HP foster it: you can't wander around long in the Palo Alto facilities without seeing lots of people sitting

together in rooms with blackboards, working casually on problems. Any one of those ad hoc meetings is likely to include people from R & D, manufacturing, engineering, marketing, and sales. That's in marked contrast to most large companies we've worked with, where the managers and analysts never meet or talk to customers, never meet or talk to salesmen, and never look at or touch the product (and the word "never" is not chosen lightly).

One of my mentors, leadership expert John C. Maxwell, used to call it "walking slowly through the crowd." Senior leaders are always going somewhere; they're often in a hurry. They're walking by key people in their organization, and while they're cordial and polite and acknowledge the people they pass in the hallway, often they're moving so fast, the casual "Hi. How are you today?" is all they have time for.

John taught me that when I am in that mode, I am missing opportunities to affect and impact individual lives as well as the life of the organization.

Walk . . . slowly . . . through . . . the . . . crowd.

Notice people, talk with them,

listen to them,

and,

oh yes—share the vision.

These occasions offer you valuable opportunities to casually talk about the company's direction and destination. Where you're headed—and how the journey's going. You get a chance to take off the title and just be you. Connecting on a personal level with your people engages them with the vision and the day-to-day initiatives more effectively than any carefully crafted speech to the group.

If you don't already do this, try it when you get to the office tomorrow. Schedule a half hour to just wander around your company. And when you do, walk slowly. Talk to people, ask questions, let them ask you questions, and encourage, challenge, and remind them of where you're going. Remind them what the destination is.

2. Communicate in as Many Ways as You Can

One of the most important messages you will communicate to the people in your company is your destination. It would be easier if that was the only message they hear in a day. While experts disagree as to the actual number of advertising messages a person is bombarded with every day, most put it between 3,000 and 5,000.[4] To say your message has some competition is to grossly undersell the reality.

To take it a step farther, hearing the same message in the same way and the same medium day after day also limits its effectiveness. You need to find a way to overcome "message fatigue."

Creativity will help you communicate your direction message. Find people in your organization who are creative and who understand the direction and vision. Sit down with them and give them permission to come up with the most creative and fun ways to communicate the answer to the question, "Where are we going?"

I'm with you—"corporate speak" is often boring, but it does not have to be. In fact, if you want to take your company to the destination you have chosen, it better not be boring. Surround yourself with creative people. Give them permission and the authority to craft the message. Turn them loose and watch what will happen across your organization when the people you lead get the picture. It makes a difference.

If you take the same route to work every day, you drive by signs and billboards every workday of your life. After a while, you don't even notice them—until they change. Why do you notice them? Because they are different—and the new message, or the same message given in a different way, grabs your attention.

Describe your destination—where you're going and what you want to accomplish—in as many different ways as possible.

3. Communicate It in as Much Detail as You Can

If you're not a natural communicator, invest the time in shaping your message. Get help with your communication skills if you need it; it's worth the time.

The tour guide I met in Chicago talked with such specificity about the vision of her company that I knew the CEO (and her immediate supervisors) had communicated the direction message in great detail. And, it had made a difference as it moved through the channels of communication. She had internalized it; she owned it.

Your job is to say to your people, "See that mountain over there? We're going to climb that mountain. And here's what it's going to be like. On the way up, we'll encounter challenges and maybe even some obstacles. But we're good; we have the tools and abilities necessary to get to the top. And when we get to the top, you can't even begin to understand how great it's going to be. We'll be able to accomplish this. And here's what you'll experience."

Does that kind of communication come naturally? Probably not. Does it take some work? Yes. Is it worth the time and effort? Definitely. Here's why: 1) Because it's motivating. 2) Because it reminds the person they are not alone; they are part of a group of dedicated individuals working together to do something special.

4. Communicate It as Specifically as You Can

Along with descriptively communicating the direction, you will need to be as specific as you possibly can. We'll talk more about this later in the book when we talk about the endgame. But specificity is important. And, like the description above, it can be motivating as well.

Let's say you're taking your young children on a driving trip to California. I can guarantee that more than once you will hear things like, "Are we there yet?" "How much longer?" Can I say, "Been there, done that"?

Do you know what might help? Using words like palm trees, ocean, the beach, Hollywood, Beverly Hills (if they're a little older), and Universal Studios will help them. Those are all specific things they will get to see when you finally arrive. And Disneyland. Yes, Disneyland always helps. (Save that one for last.) You've just helped your young passenger because you've described the destination; you've created a sense of anticipation. We're going somewhere and when we get there, it's going to be fantastic.

Let's say you're not leading an organization right now. You're where I was a few years ago, wondering what is next in your career development. Perhaps you've decided that it's time to make a midcourse career change.

You're asking the question, "What now?" What shape will your new vocation take? Where will this new leap take you? Or maybe, what will be the dream that occupies the second half of your life?

A ONE-ON-ONE COACHING SESSION WITH DAVE

If you and I had a chance to sit down in your office, we could explore all kinds of possibilities. I would do some of my favorite things: I would ask you questions and then listen to you dream out loud. We could be talking about you as an individual, or about your company's destination. The questions can be very similar and the process works the same.

I'd ask:

- What have you always dreamed about doing?

- If you knew you could accomplish anything without fear of failure, what would you try?

- If you wanted to become someone new or do something different, what would you become?

- What needs do you see that you could help alleviate?

- And, in relation to the previous question, what pain or problem do you have the skills and abilities to help or solve?

If you want to make a difference or live a life of significance, the perfect place can often be found at the intersection of your desires and the needs of the world.

One of my favorite writers, Frederick Buechner, says it beautifully: "The place God calls you to is the place where your deep gladness and the world's deep hunger meet."[5]

Sooner or later we'd get to the question, "What do you want?" Not your wife, not your kids, not your parents, not your brother, not your boss, not your next-door neighbor. What do *you* want? What do *you* really want?"

When we get to that question, there's one more thing I'd tell you in our coaching session:

It took me quite a while for that reality to sink into my own consciousness before I could pass it on to others. As strange as it may seem, I didn't know I had the freedom to choose.

While I was in the midst of trying to figure out what was next for me, I attended a conference. The host for our two days together began each session with some motivational quip or story or experience from his own extremely successful career. Apparently he sensed that there were others like me struggling with thinking they needed someone's approval or permission to pursue their dreams. It was like he read our minds, for regularly and rhythmically throughout those two days, he just kept repeating the mantra, "You don't have to ask for permission."

That was huge for me. Until that moment, I did not realize that was even a possibility. It set me free—and I want it to set you free, too.

You don't need anyone else's permission to pursue what you truly desire.

Finally, I would encourage you to find various ways to communicate your new direction to yourself. And, just as I have suggested to those who are leading an organization, find a way to communicate it to yourself whenever you can . . . as often as you can . . . in as many ways as you can . . . as descriptively as you can . . . as specifically as you can . . . and as creatively as you can.

Write down the messages you need to hear and read them often. Say them out loud if you need to. Put reminders on your desk. I like to laminate things; for whatever reason, if I laminate it, it takes on greater significance. Whatever works for you, employ it to remind you of your new destination, for you've just answered a very important question: "Where am I going?"

To remind you that you don't need anyone's permission to pursue what you truly desire, download a wallpaper for your iPhone or computer at IntentionalLeadershiptheBook. com/wallpaper.

2

WHAT'S THE WHY?

People don't buy what you do, they buy why you do it.

—Simon Sinek

One Sunday afternoon, we had gathered some of the senior leadership team at our house just to hang out. It was a time for some well-deserved relaxation and fun—out of the office and away from work.

Still, as is often the case, the conversation turned to work. So I thought I would take the opportunity to float some ideas. I wanted to give them an inside peek into some of the things I was thinking. Some ideas for new initiatives, some changes I thought might be in order, areas where I thought we could make a concerted effort to improve.

You might say I was floating a couple of test balloons. The quizzical looks on various faces indicated I had caught a couple of them by surprise. It wasn't a big deal—no decisions had been made. We were just talking.

As the afternoon wore on and side conversations began to develop, my wife happened upon one of those conversations. Sensing some concern in the voices of our trusted staff, Kathy sought to reassure them.

"Don't worry," she said. "David always has a reason for everything he does."

Then to further assure them she added, "Sometimes it's a stupid reason. But there is always a reason."

She was right—guilty as charged. I always had a reason. And while I might not think the ideas were stupid (thanks for the vote of confidence, dear), sometimes the reasoning was a little light on logic.

I always had a reason, because early in my leadership career I learned that the question of *why* was pretty important. In fact, though the question of *where* appears first in this book, in my mind, the question of *why* is equally as important.

Whether it is in my own life or in the life of my organization, I have to answer the question, "Where am I going?" But right on the heels of that, I need to be able to answer the question, "Why am I going there?"

WHY THE WHY IS SO IMPORTANT

Simon Sinek has written the definitive work on the importance of the *why*. In his words, "By WHY I mean what is your purpose, cause or belief? WHY does your company exist? WHY do you get out of bed every morning? And WHY should anyone care?"[6]

To go back to the target that Charlie Brown drew on the fence earlier in this book, Sinek has created his own target—what he calls "The Golden Circle."

The outermost circle is represented by *what*. According to Sinek, this is your job title or function. The *what* represents the product you sell or the service you offer. In his model, Sinek asserts that *everyone* knows what their job is.

The circle immediately to the inside of the *what* is the *how*. According to Sinek, *some people* know *how* they do what they do. As he said, *"Whether you call them a 'differentiating value proposition,' 'proprietary process' or 'unique selling proposition,' HOWs are* often given to explain how something is different or better."

But, according to Sinek, *very few people* know *why* they do what they do. He wrote that the one missing detail was: "WHY: Very few people or companies can clearly articulate WHY they do WHAT they do. WHY is not about making money—that's a result."

And your *why* is where you start.

I wholeheartedly endorse what Simon Sinek has proposed. He has covered the issue profoundly. As it applies to intentional leadership, I would add that there are at least five reasons why this question of *why* is so important:

- It helps you handle adversity
- It provides inspiration

- It provides motivation

- It helps maintain focus

- It helps to overcome vision leak

The Why Helps You Handle Adversity and Overcome Obstacles

I made the case in the introduction that while leadership may not be complicated, it is not easy. Quite the contrary—leadership is incredibly difficult. Perhaps at no time is it more difficult than when you or your company are trying to take new ground, chart a new course, or head in a new direction. The road is rarely smooth, but never is it more difficult than during these significant endeavors.

If you're leading yourself in a new direction, you must develop new habits . . . or eliminate old ones. You may be going in a direction that causes the learning curve to be a little steep. If you're starting a new business, establishing it and getting it going takes time and money—both of which are often in short supply at the beginning.

I recently read the story of the birth of Google. It captured beautifully the stress and pressure that Larry Page and Sergey Brin endured as they chased their crazy idea.

Brin and Page "quickly discovered that search engines require an extraordinary amount of computing resources. They didn't have the money to buy new computers, so they begged and borrowed Google into existence . . . "—including maxing out their credit cards to buy enough hard drives to basically contain the Web.[7]

One of my neighbors and I share the commonality of both starting companies. So from time to time we'll talk together, or I should say commiserate together, because starting a company is hard work. I remember a conversation from early on where he told me they were in their fifth year and expected they, for the first time, would show a profit.

I felt the relief in his voice. My company was in the black at that moment, but just barely. My neighbor and I would agree: It is wonderfully exciting to start your own company, but it is excruciatingly hard—which is why so many new businesses fail so quickly. It is estimated that 50 percent of new companies survive the first four or five years. But by the time they reach the ten-year mark, 96 percent of them will have succumbed.[8]

It's incredibly hard. Startups represent the perfect storm of adversity and obstacles.

If this describes you, more than once you will ask yourself, "Now why am I doing this again?" You're not alone. Your fellow entrepreneurs often ask themselves that same question.

That's why the question of *why* is so important. That's why Simon Sinek says *why* is where you need to start. I've often said that there are times when the *why* is all you have. Nothing else may seem to be working, but at least you know *why* you're trying.

Established companies, however, often fare no better when they're going through major directional changes—establishing a new product, rebranding the company, starting a new division or shutting one down in order to make the company more effective and profitable, or trying to staff a new department. These kinds of challenges are neither easy nor allow you to sleep restfully at night.

There are two things I know about trying to grow something. One, you will experience adversity, and two, you will encounter obstacles to overcome. Therefore, the answer to the question of *why* needs to be solid.

Why plays a role in individual endeavors as well. As I write this, my friend is training for a marathon at the end of the month. The purpose of the marathon is to raise funds to help support orphans in India with HIV/AIDS. It's an incredibly worthwhile cause. I've never trained for a marathon, but I know my friend goes on many early morning training runs, sometimes in the dark, sometimes in chilly temperatures, and often alone. There are long weekend runs of thirteen, fourteen, eighteen, or even twenty miles. I imagine she often asks herself why she is enduring all this misery. And in the midst of a long training run in the dark on a Saturday morning, she reminds herself there is a child in India with a horrendous disease and no parents, who depends on her to put in those miles. That's the *why*—and she runs on.

Knowing your *why* goes a long way toward helping you handle any amount of adversity and overcome the obstacles that will surely come your way.

The Why *Provides Inspiration–to You and Others*

I find my friend's endeavor to run her marathon extremely inspirational. So much so that I want to join her in this project. No, I won't be running the 26.2 miles, but I want to do whatever

I can to support what she is doing. My wife and I will no doubt join the team that financially supports the cause she represents.

You might say that her *why* has become a *why* for us. Until a year ago, I didn't know this organization existed.[9] Finding out about what they're doing, however, and knowing someone who is participating in it has transferred the *why* to me. And it goes farther—my wife is thinking about running next year.

Why can become contagious.

Remember the tour guide I mentioned earlier? When she guided us around the campus and told us stories about the trials and successes of her company, I was struck by how much she owned the direction *and* the *why*. In fact, at one moment when she told us about a rather impressive moment of success, she looked at me and the rest of my group and said, "This is why we do what we do."

In another setting we might say, "She had caught the vision." While that is true, more specifically, she owned the *why*. Somewhere the CEO had shared the *why* with a board of directors. It had inspired them enough to say, "We're with you; let's go for it." Then the direction and destination was communicated to the rest of the organization, and they owned it. Eventually the direction and the *why* were communicated to someone who was simply giving a tour to some visitors—and the *why* grabbed her to the point that the organization's *why* had become her *why*. So with passion and pride that day, she didn't refer to her company or to the CEO or to her boss. She said, "This is why *we* do what we do."

Why always brings inspiration.

The **Why** *Provides Motivation*

There's an old story about a construction project in New York City. A reporter was putting together a piece on the project and asked a couple of the workers who were nearby what they were doing.

One worker said he was just doing his job, hauling bricks and mixing cement so the bricklayers could build one of the walls of a new building.

The reporter asked the same question of another worker and he responded, "I'm building a brand new, beautiful cathedral where people will be able to come and worship God."

Which worker do you think was probably going to do a better job? Which worker was going to more successfully handle adversity and overcome obstacles in the completion of the project? Which worker was more inspired? Which worker was more motivated?

Of course, the second one. Why? Because he understood the *why*. The first worker was building a building. It was another job, just like the one before that and the one before that. He would build another building when this one was finished.

The second worker was not just building a building. He was building a beautiful and glorious cathedral. Because he knew the *why*, the second worker was motivated to do his part, to do the best he could, to make sure the project was completed and lived up to its *why*.

Motivation is undeniably important and much is written about it. Google the word and you'll be reading for days. Perhaps the great Les Brown said it best:

Wanting something is not enough. You must hunger for it. Your motivation must be absolutely compelling in order to overcome the obstacles that will invariably come your way.

Brown is talking about the *why*—and he's right.

The Why *Helps Maintain Focus*

Focus is a popular subject today. It occupies endless blog pieces, magazine articles, and even workshops, seminars, webinars, and conferences. Perhaps to be more correct, what truly dominates the airwaves and Internet are articles about what interferes with focus—distraction. How to maintain focus, how not to yield to distractions, and how to counter the reality that we are perhaps the most distracted society in history. And it's not just a personal issue, it's also a company-wide issue of distraction.

A recent article from *Entrepreneur* magazine states that I need to focus on top clients. Michael Hyatt teaches me seven ways to get super-focused when I really need it. Jeff Goins has insights to help me stay more focused when I'm writing. And James Clear has suggestions for me on how to stay focused when I'm bored.

The problem of focus is an epidemic in today's marketplace, but it is not a new problem. It's as Stephen R. Covey stated:

The main thing is to keep the main thing the main thing.

This problem has always plagued humanity. The temptation on the part of both individuals and corporations is to become distracted by trying to do more and more as they grow more successful.

Eventually, the original or main focus often becomes blurred, and slowly—without even realizing it—they have moved away from their strengths, their main focus, and sometimes even their core competencies. Over time, their effectiveness wanes and, unwittingly, they have put their future success and even survival in jeopardy.

That's why the *why* is so important—it helps maintain focus.

One of the reasons my own endeavors took longer than I expected was distraction. There was such a plethora of options and I had many interests. So many that nailing down the ultimate destination and the reason *why* grew more difficult and complicated over time. Thankfully, with the help of some dear friends and trusted confidants, I got through that season. The result is a much keener and more refined focus than I possessed earlier.

However, even now I fight the distraction battle constantly. Questions like these continue to plague me.

- What areas of leadership and business do I want to consult in?

- What kinds of executives do I want to coach?

- In what specialties can I truly make a difference?

It's a process, to be sure, but what I've discovered is that a clear picture of *where* and *why*, and especially the *why*, helps me maintain better focus.

Each time new opportunities arise, I again ask myself the critical questions:

- How does this fit into my long-term direction?

- Does this match my *why*?

If the answer to both of those questions is "Yes," then the new opportunity has a chance of being considered. If the answer to just one of those questions is "No," I politely decline and move on—not looking back. (At least, that's the intent.)

If, like me, you're easily distracted, a clear understanding of your *why* is vital to your success and effectiveness, as well as lowering the stress level of your life.

The Why *Helps Overcome Vision Leak*

I don't hear many leadership experts talk about vision leak, which surprises me because it is a definite malady both at the individual and corporate level.

One of my mentors described vision leak this way: Say your life is represented by a bucket. Your organization's life can be pictured the same way. As the leader, you do everything you can to fill the members of your organization with a clear vision about *where* you're going. You paint a compelling picture of *why* you're heading in that direction. You craft an inspiring message. You're specific and creative. To be honest, it's truly motivating. But because humans are human, and your company is filled with humans, the vision leaks out. And you didn't realize there was a hole in the bottom of the bucket. That's not some sinister plot. No evil ninja put the hole there; life put the hole there. Everyone's life is filled with, well, everything else.

The people in your company have lives filled with activities, obligations, families, bills to pay, soccer games to attend, kids to get through school, vacations to take, aging parents to tend to, and an unending list of things all competing for time, attention, and energy.

This reality is not an extraordinary anomaly—it's life. No one needs to get a life—everyone has a life. And with that life comes obligations and commitments, all of which contribute to vision leak. Incidentally, this reality is also why you need to communicate the direction whenever you can, as often as you can. The same principle applies to communicating the *why*.

There's an ancient story that, I think, illustrates this beautifully. The ancient Israelites had been invaded and hauled off into captivity and slavery. Their capital city, Jerusalem, (to the people of Israel, a sacred city) had been destroyed along with the mighty walls around the city.

One of those prisoners of war was a young leader named Nehemiah. His role as prisoner was to serve the king. He was inspired to go back and inspect the ruins of his capital city. Miraculously, the king granted him permission and Nehemiah took a group of fellow prisoners back to Jerusalem to inspect the devastation that had befallen their precious city.

Heartbroken and sickened by the devastation of this once great place, Nehemiah sought and was again miraculously granted permission, this time to assemble a crew of skilled laborers and craftsman to go back to Jerusalem and at least rebuild the walls around the city, to restore a little of its past glory and ensure that nothing else would happen to this vital piece of their homeland.

Nehemiah, an admirable and effective leader, gathered together a large group of his fellow prisoners and began to cast the vision of what he dreamed might take place.

His message to his fellow prisoners contained two vital pieces of information. This is what we're going to do (*where* are we going?). And, this is why we're going to do it (*why* are we going there?). An effective vision caster, Nehemiah had no problem inspiring his fellow slaves to sign on for the added duty. They were in. "Let's do it," they cheered. And the building project began.

According to the ancient story, rebuilding and restoring the walls was completed in 52 days—amazingly quick for such a monumental project. As often is the case, there were obstacles to overcome and obvious adversity in the process. But they handled it because they knew *why* they had undertaken this project in the first place.

But, according to the story, around day 26, about halfway through the project, the obstacles and adversity began to overcome these young builders. They began to question the purpose of what they were doing. They complained about why they had left the comfort of their homes (remember, they were slaves in captivity) to do something as foolish as rebuilding these walls. Morale began to sink, work slowed down, and a strike was being contemplated.

What had happened? The vision began to leak. The tank full of *why* was draining out.

So Nehemiah again took to vision casting and reminded his workers just *what* they were trying to accomplish. He again declared to this ad hoc organization where they were going. Further, he reminded them of the noble reasons for undertaking this endeavor. He reasserted the monumental *why* for this project. On the basis of the *where* and *why*, he again called them to action. And again, vision bucket refilled, they willingly joined in and finished the project over the next 26 days.

A casual observer who doesn't understand the process might judge the prisoners for their discouragement and lack of enthusiasm. But they weren't bad people, and neither were they problem employees. The vision bucket had gotten close to empty and needed to be refilled. That's the way life is.

Renew the vision with communication

Another of my mentors used that story to teach me that as the leader of an organization, I needed to find a way to renew the vision for my people every 26 days, or roughly once a month. I don't know if that is a hard and fast principle or not. But I do know that as a leader, I need to find a way to communicate our direction and vision as often as I can. And that part of that communication must involve an answer to the question, "*Why are we going there?*"

Renew your vision once a month.

Another equally important application for these principles is for someone who is making monumental changes in his or her personal life—you're moving in a new direction; perhaps you've left cubicle world and have decided to follow your dreams because you feel you can make a bigger difference in the world with your own entrepreneurial startup. Or, you've created a new nonprofit because you want to alleviate suffering or tend to a need that no one else seems to be addressing. Or, maybe you just want to be your own boss for once, so you've walked through the corporate turnstile for the last time.

If you're that person, I say, "Way to go!"

But I also remind you to make sure you know your *why*. All those benefits that an organization derives from knowing the *why* are also crucial to you as you embark on your new, exciting life's journey.

Undoubtedly, you will face adversity and obstacles. Your *why* will not allow you to "breeze" through them, but it will help you overcome them. Your *why* will not only inspire you, it will also inspire the people you convince to join you in your worthy endeavors. Inspiration can never be underestimated.

Your *why* will not only motivate you and your team, it will help keep you focused and help you to not succumb to the distraction machine called the world in which we live. And finally, a healthy dose of *why* helps plug the hole in your vision bucket.

The continual reminder of *why* needs to be kept in front of everyone involved in pursuing your dream.

Make sure you communicate it—and often.

COMMUNICATING THE *WHY*

You'll need to communicate your *why* often (as often as you can) and in a variety of ways. Let's talk about *when* and then *how* to communicate your *why*.

There are five strategic moments when communicating your *why* is crucial.

1. At the Beginning

When your key leaders and decision makers are sitting around that conference table and you're launching the new initiatives that will take your organization to a new level of growth, please include a section in your presentation where you discuss the *why* of these new plans.

This is crucial for at least three reasons. First, *why* provides inspiration and motivation—which helps your people overcome whatever adversity arises with this new initiative and helps them keep their focus, especially when the temptation to give up or go back to the old ways arises. Don't underestimate the power of the *why* to motivate people.

All over our country there are untold thousands of workers doing their jobs. They're making a widget, providing a service, selling a product. They're doing a good job but they don't know why they're doing it—beyond that it provides a livelihood and pays their family's bills. It's just what they do.

Second, communicate the *why* when launching new plans to provide the fuel and energy to get started. Rocket scientists can tell you exactly how much energy it takes to get a rocket off the ground—it's massive. For example, an average space shuttle flight will use around a half a million gallons of hydrogen and oxygen. But during the initial stages of lift off, the shuttle is burning its fuel at a rate of 1,000 gallons per second.[10]

The greatest amount of energy is always used at the beginning of the endeavor, just to get it going. Knowing your *why* will greatly aid the launch of your endeavor.

Third, express the *why* at the beginning of your endeavor because it's naturally going to be the first question that comes to people's minds anyway. They'll already be wondering *why*, so it's the perfect opportunity to share it.

Do you remember one of the first words your darling daughter learned without you teaching her? (Well . . . the first word was "No," but that's a different discussion.) One of the first words she learned was, "Why?" This type of conversation may sound familiar to you:

"What are you doing, Dad?"

"I'm washing the dishes, sweetie."

"Why?"

"Because they were dirty."

"Why?"

"Because we used them to eat dinner."

"Why?"

"Because we put our food on them."

"Why?"

"Because that's how we eat."

"Why?"

"Because it's better than just putting our food on the table."

"Why?"

"Because I said so."

As frustrating as it is, your child's curiosity is a wonderful thing. Sadly, many of us lose that curiosity as we grow older. I'm fairly certain, however, that when you announce that BHAG[11] (big, hairy, audacious goal) to the people in your organization, that curiosity will quickly come back.

2. At Strategic Points Along the Way

This goes back to the concept of vision leak. One of my mentors once told me that as a leader, I would need to find a way to renew the vision (both the direction and why) at least once every month.

You will have to decide how often works for your situation. I would suggest as often as you can, whenever you can. That includes informal as well as formal situations and occasions.

You're having lunch with a couple of your department heads. Talking shop is the perfect time to remind them of the *why*. You're not banging them over the head with it—you are simply "sowing seeds." You're slipping it in during a casual moment, a reminder that will come back to them later.

When you're chatting with your people during one of your new MBWA times (you have implemented "management by walking around," haven't you?), you'll often notice that you have stumbled upon the perfect time to remind people about *why* your organization is heading in its current direction.

The principle is—
when it is a natural part of **your** conversation, eventually it will become a natural part of **their** conversation.

If you're the leader who is leading yourself in a new direction personally, this principle is also crucial.

I am currently involved in some new initiatives myself, both personally and with my company. During the planning and creative stages, I completed some simple documents that remind me *where* I am going and *why* I am going there. Their importance is usually signified by the fact that they are laminated. I used to joke that if I laminate something, that means it's holy.

Reviewing those laminated cards reminds me of what I'm trying to accomplish and, yes, *why*. I try to look at them at least every couple of weeks, if not weekly. Remember, I can get easily distracted and reviewing the cards helps me maintain focus. My vision leaks, too; these documents inspire me to stay at it. I am going somewhere and this is *why*.

3. When Something Happens That Reinforces the Vision

There will be moments on your journey as an individual or an organization that will naturally serve as examples when referring to the *why* with your people.

Let's say that one of your initiatives includes doubling your revenue over the next three years. You want your small business to go from $3 million in gross annual revenue to $6 million.

With that in mind, your sales department has incorporated some new initiatives and plans to help accomplish their part of the overall company goals. Your best sales rep once again goes after the client that has eluded him. Armed with the motivation and inspiration that your beautifully and regularly communicated vision has given him, he devises a plan with a new approach.

This time around, your rep is able to move that stubborn prospect from an opportunity to a customer, and he brings back the largest contract that your company has ever landed.

Everyone is celebrating. High fives, pats on the back, and champagne (at the close of the day, of course) are in order on this momentous day. And you've joined in the celebration, as well you should.

You get everyone's attention as you raise your glass with a toast to the sales rep and the sales department, as well as the rest of the company who has gathered with you. And you remind them that this is *why* you embarked on a new journey as an organization. This is *why* you've challenged them to reach higher and dig deeper and work harder. (Okay, try not to use the clichés, but you get the point.) It's a perfect opportunity to remind them of the *why*.

4. When Reaching Milestones

When you and your team embarked on this new journey to a new destination, you undoubtedly put together a plan as to how you would get there.

Certainly you put on the wall certain milestones that would indicate your progress. Let's stick with the goal to double your revenue in three years, as an example.

You planned to grow your revenue by 25 percent at the end of the first year, with another 35 percent by the end of year two, before blowing the doors off with a whopping 40 percent in the final year.

When the numbers come in after the first year, you discover that you actually grew your gross revenue over the past year by 26 percent. You're on target—you're well on your way to arriving at your destination, and on time. Let's celebrate—you've reached one of your first milestones. While you're congratulating everyone for their hard work and dedication, don't forget to remind them *why* they're dedicated and working so hard.

Celebrating milestones along the way is crucial to long-term success. And those milestone celebrations provide the perfect opportunity to again sow the seeds of vision and direction as well as the *why* of what you're doing. Believe me, they will go a long way toward building morale and growing inspiration and motivation, as well as recalibrating a laser-like focus for your organization.

5. When You Arrive

It should go without saying that when you arrive at your destination, it should be the biggest party and celebration of all.

Notice, I said, "should go without saying." If you're like me, you may forget that. Several years ago, I discovered an innate condition in my psyche that I came to call being "joy challenged." I tend to be so focused on what's next that often I fail to stop and celebrate the progress and accomplishment that we've already experienced.

I realized this malady one night in a startling way. The organization I was leading at the time had completed a multimillion dollar building program a year or so before my moment of enlightenment. If you've ever built anything, you know the work involved. Casting vision, raising money, motivating sacrifice, securing permits and permission, developing architectural plans, breaking ground, watching the progress that is always slower than you want.

But there is that moment when everything is in place—it's finished. Then comes the grand opening and the dedication ceremony, as well as getting used to your new home and surroundings.

Our construction project included a brand new, state-of-the-art auditorium with all the bells and whistles you could imagine. It was a beautiful room . . . only I had never really stopped to notice. As is my nature, I had automatically moved on to "what's next?"

One night, my wife and I attended an event being held there for which I had no responsibility. We were just participants. I sat there and found myself looking around the room and, for the first time since we had moved in, I began to notice how beautiful it was. I elbowed my wife.

"This is a beautiful room," I whispered.

"Yes, it is."

I continued to look around, having long ago abandoned what was happening on stage. I elbowed her again.

"What?!?!" she whispered with an annoying glance.

"This is *really* a beautiful room."

She seemed confused . . . annoyingly confused. But I had just realized an important reality. In all the work and effort to accomplish the goal, with all the time and energy and money spent to reach our destination, I had never stopped to enjoy or truly celebrate arriving at where we were going.

When you get to where you're going as an organization, when you've reached your destination goal, it's not time to rest or sit back, but don't forget to celebrate what you've accomplished.

And when you celebrate, it's the perfect time to remind them one more time of the *why* that has driven you all the way.

We've talked about when to communicate the *why*, let's wrap this up with *how* to do it.

We live in a wonderful time—a time when the incredible technological advances we enjoy provide us with a seemingly unending list of options and methods to make communication more effective and inspiring. What's available to you today has the potential to provide incredible inspiration and motivation through stories, videos, pictures, and testimonials.

I'm coming to understand the importance of stories. Stories have the power to inspire, teach, motivate, focus, equip, and bring about change.

Some of you reading this book were not yet born when one of the most significant events in our nation's history took place. I'm referring to the march on Washington in 1963 where, on the mall in front of the Lincoln Memorial, Dr. Martin Luther King delivered his immortal "I Have a Dream" speech.

It was officially billed as the March on Washington for Jobs and Freedom. King had struggled and labored long on this important speech. In fact, when he arrived in Washington the night before the march, he still didn't have a complete draft. He stayed up most of the night writing the final draft, finishing around four in the morning.

The phrase "I have a dream" would not be found in that draft. He had used the phrase in other presentations but King didn't think he would have time for it in this speech.[12]

It was a long afternoon program filled with songs and speeches. Dr. King was last on the program. At one point people got up, began to pack up and leave. They had traveled by buses, trains, and cars for days. They were tired and wanted to go home.

Then Mahalia Jackson got up to sing—and everything changed. The people "heading for the exits" stopped and the stage was set for Dr. King's presentation.

King read from his prepared text quoting the Bible, the Constitution, and the Declaration of Independence. He was moving toward his conclusion, in fact skipping some of the parts that had been written down.

Standing nearby, off to the side, Mahalia Jackson shouted, "Tell them about the dream, Martin."

As he continues on, she says it again.

"Tell them about the dream, Martin."

I don't know how many times she said it, but it finally caught hold in King's consciousness. He later explained in an interview, "All of a sudden this thing came to me that I have used—I'd used many times before, that thing about 'I have a dream'—and I just felt that I wanted to use it here."

Jackson's words imploring him to "tell them about the dream" resonated, and Dr. King launched into the passage that would eventually change our nation's direction and path forever.

"I say to you today, my friends, so even though we face the difficulties of today and tomorrow, I still have a dream." And he was off, delivering some of the most beloved lines in American history, telling a story he never intended to tell.

The entire address on that sparkling, sunny, hot, and humid day was monumental. But in all honesty, I don't remember a lot of the words before the phrase "I have a dream" was first uttered. But what took place after those words first rang out is forever unforgettable.

It is still looked upon as a turning point for all involved.

Stories are significant. Your company is full of them. Your personal life is full of them. Inspiring stories that possess the power to produce change and motivation, stories that will help maintain focus. They're part of your history. And they're happening every day.

Here's my suggestion: Find a way to preserve and present those stories. Use any medium you can—news-letters, blog posts, videos, interviews, speeches, company podcasts, testimonials, emails, coffee chats.

Nothing is better employed to communicate the *why* than to tell the stories that make up the fabric of your organization or your life. Find the most creative people in your company that you can and turn them loose to create something that will motivate and inspire your people with the *why* of where you're going as a company.

The collaboration and results will help develop a sense of teamwork and camaraderie, and will build a strong sense of unity as your team moves toward your chosen destination.

3

WHAT'S THE PLAN?

A vision, without a plan, is just a hallucination.

—Will Rogers

While Will Rogers' snappy wit gets credit for the above saying, it's actually a variation of an old, old proverb, which states:

A vision without a plan is just a dream.
A plan without a vision is just drudgery.
But a vision with a plan can change
the world.

I may be suffering "delusions of grandeur," but I want to change the world. Most entrepreneurs do. Thus, it is more than just prudent to, once you have discovered your *where* and formulated your *why*, next put a plan in place.

THE IMPORTANCE OF A PLAN

There are several reasons why having a plan to reach your destination is so imperative.

A Plan Makes the Where Possible

It's one thing to have a clear destination in mind. It's even better to have a burning *why* within to motivate you on your way to where you want to go. But if you don't have a plan for getting there, you will never arrive. And that is not hyperbole. You don't get anywhere by accident—certainly nowhere significant.

In other words, say you do want to change the world. Great—how are you going to do it? What's the plan—what methods, tools, and tactics will you use? What's your strategy?

Many have visions—even more have dreams. But it is those who put a definite and strategic plan in place who see their visions realized and their dreams come true.

A Plan Reduces Frustration

Not everything will go smoothly. And, as I have learned (much to my regret), often things take longer than they should.

Again, one of the benefits of knowing your *why* is that it helps you deal with adversity and overcome obstacles: adversity *will* occur.

There are two kinds of people in the world: those who have problems and those who are about to have problems. For either group, the chance of frustration runs high.

Having a plan helps reduce the frustration. When you have a plan in place, there is no need to panic. Why? You know what to do next. An added benefit is—if following your plan reduces your need to panic, those traveling with you will not find the need to panic either.

A Plan Helps You Retain Employees

If you don't have a plan, there's a good chance that your people will find other things to do or other places to work.

Let's unpack this a bit.

Those following your leadership will often deal with their frustration by leaving. If, as their leader, you have not firmly and confidently communicated the plan for getting to your declared destination, their frustration will increase—problems will appear more quickly and people will not have the tools to fix the difficulties.

Robert E. Quinn, who I noted earlier, also points out in his book, *Deep Change*, that people easily recognize when "critical issues" are being ignored. Quinn writes, "When someone makes the initial decision to avoid confronting a difficult situation, a negative process is triggered. The person becomes deeply frustrated and eventually quits trying."

He points out that part of the "negative process" that has been triggered includes workers feeling like victims—powerless to have any kind of positive effect or outcome. He also connects the role of the victim to consciously choosing destructive paths rather than trying to initiate change.

If you cannot reduce this frustration, there is a good chance people will find other things to do while working for you. And, if the frustration continues to mount, chances are they will find someplace else to report each week, a place where their minds and hearts can be challenged and where their valuable skills and talents can be fully utilized.

Having a frustrated team is a recipe for disaster. I have witnessed this firsthand. Several years ago when I had first arrived at a new opportunity, I had the privilege of reuniting with an associate with whom I had worked several years before in a different organization. We had developed a great friendship and had worked together successfully. Our friendship, familiarity, and knowledge of each other's strengths and style would be very useful and of great benefit.

There was only one problem. I had just come out of a very difficult situation and, admittedly, was somewhat reticent to act on a couple of issues and put specific plans in place to ensure forward movement.

He thought this was very unlike me—and he was right. Because he didn't know the reason for the change or the lack of definitive action, his frustration began to mount, so much so that he finally had to confront me.

I still remember the day he walked into my office, shut the door, sat down in front of my desk, looked me in the eye, and asked, "What is your problem?" He was neither belligerent nor insubordinate nor disrespectful. He was a friend and associate needing an answer as to why his leader didn't have a plan to get to where we had together decided we were going.

For me, it was a wake-up call. I'd better get busy, for certainly the frustration my friend was feeling was being felt by others as well. We knew where we were going—we knew why. But I hadn't put a plan in place for getting there. That leads to the final reason why a plan is so important.

A Plan Helps Maintain Momentum

In the situation I just described, my friend's frustration led to a difficult conversation on his part—with me. But out of that conversation came a plan to create a plan. As a result, two significant things happened: 1) his frustration subsided, and 2) we were able to create significant momentum that took us a long way toward our established destination and direction.

The suggestions below come from that experience—it is exactly what we did to resolve the frustration. And, at the end of the process, our organization had a plan in place and we were well on our way to the determined destination. The company thrived, revenue increased greatly, and momentum grew to an all-time high.

That is the benefit of having a plan.

HOW TO CREATE THE PLAN

Creating your plan is not a complicated process. It really isn't. But it takes time, patience, guidance, and leadership. That's where you—the leader—need to be strong. By strong I don't mean autocratic or controlling. This is where you need to be a strong leader by being an excellent guide.

Let's talk about the three steps to creating a simple but powerful plan:

1. Determine where you are
2. Get the right people in the room and decide what you will do
3. Decide what you *won't* do

Start by Determining Where You Are

It almost seems superfluous to say it, but at the risk of sounding addle, let me overstate the obvious:

You will never get to where you want to go unless you first know where you are.

Let's say you, personally, want to go to Chicago. What route will you take? That depends on where you are when you start. Clearly, the plan for getting to Chicago is different if you start from Los Angeles than it is if you start from Miami. The same is true for your company. Where you are right now plays a huge role in determining the plan for where you are trying to go.

A few years ago, my wife and I traveled to Spokane, Washington, for some regional corporate meetings. Some dear friends invited us to stay with them in their home in the country. So after our first day's schedule concluded, my wife and I made our way to our friends' home. Another couple had also been invited to join us, so we relaxed and enjoyed the evening prior to a second long day of meetings and assignments.

The next morning at breakfast, our hosts, who had to leave early for some final meeting preparations, wanted to make sure we knew how to get to the meeting site from their home. I hadn't a clue but the other couple assured us that they knew how to get there. Certain that we were taken care of, our hosts left us to find our way.

Together, we determined that my wife and I would follow the other couple in our rental car. We figured it would take about 30 to 40 minutes to get to our destination. Everything was all set—so we thought.

We had been driving for about twenty minutes, and I had this nagging sensation that we were not traveling in the right direction. In fact, it seemed to me we were no closer to our final destination than when we had started. Indeed, it felt to me that we were farther away. My gut feeling said we were going deeper and deeper into the wilderness, and I was growing more and more alarmed at the possibility that we would be terribly late to our appointments.

We kept driving. At thirty minutes, we were no closer to our destination. It became obvious that our friends in the lead car really didn't know where they were going at all. My frustration and panic grew by the minute and I had given up all hope of arriving at our destination on time and began dreading the thought of walking in late.

Seeking to help, my wife asked the obvious question, "Can't we call someone for directions?"

"No."

"Why not?"

"Do you know where we are?"

"No."

"Neither do I."

How would we be able to get directions to where we wanted to go if we had no clue where we were?

I still don't know how we finally found our way there. Needless to say, I learned several lessons that day, but that's a discussion for another time.

The appropriate lesson for us at this time is, you can't get to where you want to go unless you know where you are. That's the first step in creating your plan.

Get the Right People in the Room and Decide What You Will Do

Once you know where you are, you can begin to formulate your plan for getting where you want to go. And that's where the fun really begins.

I'm a visionary—but I'm also a strategic thinker. I can think of very few things in leadership that are more fun and exciting than getting in a room with the right people and spending a couple of days brainstorming and strategizing about all the possible ways to achieve the dream that we as an organization have chosen. For me, it is sheer joy.

In fact, as one of my dearest friends likes to say, "It's easier than breathing."

Notice I said that you must have "the right people in the room." This is a crucial. I also used that phrase when discussing how to determine the destination and direction. You need the right people in the room to accomplish that task as well—and while many of those may be the same people, you will need to include some critical additional people for creating the plan.

For the first step (determining destination/direction), you need leaders, decision makers, and influencers. You want influential people who will be able to carry the ball and communicate the dynamic vision to the rest of the organization in such a way that they can secure willing participation.

The critical additional people you need to make the plan include the strategists and tacticians who will carry the majority of the weight and responsibility for implementing the plan. Who better to create the plan than the ones who will execute it?

John Maxwell, the mentor I mentioned earlier, told me that decisions about solutions are best made at the lowest possible level. I learned that principle from him early in my leadership career, and it has served me well. More than once, I have had to fight for it when some well-meaning but misinformed senior executive thought she knew better how to do something than the one who was experienced at doing it.

Early on in my career, I was leading a very small organization. We were growing and the growth of the company necessitated that we purchase a new phone system. This was shortly after the government breakup of Ma Bell, so you know that it was quite a while ago.

The breakup of this behemoth phone company birthed smaller phone companies, and each one was eager to sell us their systems. As I interviewed various vendors I was struck by one in particular. I asked the representative, who happened to be one of the partners in this startup phone company, why he and his partner had decided to break out on their own rather than stay where they were.

He detailed for me a long list of frustrations that he and his partner had experienced for years as they had tried to faithfully deliver to the customer what the executives and sales reps had promised from the comfort of their cozy home office. Not only could he not fulfill what was promised, often what was guaranteed was impossible. In short, it just couldn't be done.

When the opportunity to break away and move out on their own presented itself, they jumped at the chance because, for once, they would be able to make legitimate and reasonable guarantees and then deliver to the customer exactly what was promised. Why? Because they were the ones making the promise and they knew what could and could not be done.

By the way, that was the company I went with and we became one of their most loyal and satisfied customers.

What are the initiatives that you are trying to accomplish? Get the people in the room who will be delivering on the promises and let them help you come up with the plan to improve and expand. Listen to them—utilize them. Give them permission to dream and create with you. Your initiatives will stand a much better chance of being realistic, practical, and achievable.

Decide What You Won't Do

Part of the planning process requires some difficult decisions. Once you have the ideas and possibilities for how to get to the chosen destination, you have to pick one. It's your classic good news/bad news situation. The good news is that your team will come up with endless possibilities of what can be done. The bad news is that your team will come up with endless possibilities of what can be done. And that's a problem.

No individual or organization can do everything. It isn't wise, possible, or profitable. That means it will be crucial during this process that you lead your team through the difficult task of deciding not only what you will do but what you won't do.

I have to continually remind myself that Warren Buffett is right. "The difference between successful people and very successful people," he once said, "is that very successful people say no to almost everything."

Here also is where the advice of master teacher Jim Collins is most potent. In his acclaimed work *Good to Great*, Collins introduces us to what he calls "The Hedgehog Concept."[13]

In his words, for a company "to go from good to great requires a deep understanding of three intersecting circles, which translate into a simple, crystalline concept (the Hedgehog Concept)."

Those three circles are:

1. What you are deeply passionate about

2. What you are the best in the world at

3. What drives your economic engine

Collins teaches that the key to the Hedgehog Concept is for your company to understand what it can be the best at as well as to know what it cannot be the best at.

Collins makes it clear that the Hedgehog Concept is not a goal or strategy—it is simply an understanding. It is an understanding that will help you as your team filters through all the ideas, strategies, tactics, and goals that result from your planning session.

Perhaps the best way to go about this is to create a matrix that employs the three questions of the Hedgehog Concept as they apply to your organization: 1) What are we deeply passionate about? 2) What can we be the best in the world at? 3) What drives our economic engine?

Remember, Collins says that your focus needs to be where all three of the circles intersect. And that "good-to-great companies set their goals and strategies based on [this] understanding."

He continues. "The good-to-great companies are more like hedgehogs—simple, dowdy creatures that know 'one big thing' and stick to it."

To help bring about the successful execution of this concept, Collins suggests a novel idea: that each company create a "stop doing list." In other words, list those things your company *won't* do. They may be things you used to do, but because of this new understanding, you will stop doing them.

To do this successfully will require possibly changing the culture of your organization. It will require you to fill the culture with self-disciplined people who will "go to extreme lengths" to fulfill their responsibilities in helping the organization reach its destination.

I can tell you from my experience that this can be massively difficult to do. For those involved, the more that is on the line in terms of "turf" and "ownership," the more demanding of you it will be to lead those people with intention.

One of the greatest examples of this comes from a story that Henry Cloud tells in his book *9 Things You Simply Must Do.*[14] In addition to being a clinical psychologist, Dr. Cloud is also a leadership expert with an established consulting practice that regularly works with leaders in Fortune 25 and Fortune 500 companies.

From that context, he tells the story of a client and friend who owns a substantial manufacturing company with annual profits in the hundreds of millions of dollars. However, it wasn't always this way.

When he took over the company it was about one-sixteenth the size it is now. Still, with annual profits in the millions of dollars, the company was considered a substantial success. After Dr. Cloud's friend took over the company, it literally exploded in growth. The company's annual profits exceeded its original sales. In Cloud's words, "It was quite an accomplishment, and he has become a recognized leader in his industry, receiving many awards for the innovative things he has done." As a result, he continues, "Many now turn to him to learn his business and leadership practices."

So what did he do to transform the company into the amazingly successful giant it became?

In the executive's own words: "I sold off 80 percent of the company at big losses when I first took it over."

Dr. Cloud's response was what yours (and mine) is. "What? How do you gut a profitable company by giving most of it away at substantial losses, and then expect it to explode?"

The executive responded, "I looked at everything the company was doing. It was making money, but the more I analyzed things, I could see that the life of the company was really in about 20 percent of its overall activity. Although the rest of it was okay, I thought it was a drain and a distraction from where the real life of the company was. The real potential was in that 20 percent that I decided to keep.

"So I sold off the rest of the operations and assets, sometimes at pennies on the dollar. I wanted to get them off our plates, out of our hair, out of our lives, and keep them from draining focus, energy, resources, and attention from the good stuff. So, I got rid of all of it. Quickly. And that move enabled us to get focused on the really good things that we had going. And this is what led to our eventual success."

Please go back and read the above story again . . . slowly. And let the words sink in. Then, put this book down for a few moments and examine everything you are doing. If you're leading an organization, review everything that it is doing.

What do you need to get rid of right now—at any cost—so that you can get to where you're going?

This is a truism that, apparently, you can take to the bank: Do you want to successfully get to where you're going? Decide what you won't do.

COMMUNICATE THE PLAN

Once you have figured out where you are as a company or an individual, and once you have gotten the right people in the room and decided what you will and will not do, it's time to communicate to the rest of your teams the plan that will be put in place to get you to where you are wanting to go.

Just as with the destination decision—the *where*—there are a variety of ways you can communicate it. Find a method of communication or reminders that fits with your organization and your teams. Put the plan where it will continually be in front of your people's eyes.

Just as you've gone to great lengths to communicate to your people *where* you're going as an organization, and you've taken the time to inspire them with the *why* that is motivating your company, let them know what plan you have in place to guarantee you will get to your desired location.

A definite plan is what makes the *where* possible. It will help reduce frustration when difficulties creep up. Not only will it help solve problems, it will provide a much-needed injection of motivation that will greatly help your team achieve your organization's goals.

Nailing down the *how* will help make the *where* a reality and possibly even change the world.

WHAT TO DO WITH THE PLAN

Do you realize how far you've come already in this process? Whether you're leading your organization or you're embarking on a new journey as an entrepreneur or leader, you've established a clear direction. You've answered the question, "Where are we going?" or "Where am *I* going?" You have a definite destination in mind.

You've also answered the clearly important question of "Why am I going there?" You're able to tell the key people in your organization why this new direction is so important.

And you've come up with a plan on how to get there. You've sat down in a room with key decision makers, influencers, and experts. You've brainstormed your way to a clear plan with workable strategies and specific and effective tactics to help you get to where you want to go or to help your company take the next steps toward even greater success.

Now what do you do with the plan? Let me suggest three uses for this planning that you and your associates have invested so much time and energy in.

Use It as a Tool to Maintain Accountability

One of the tools provided by your newly formed plan is a way to help keep everyone, including yourself, accountable for the results.

In his book *The Success System That Never Fails*, W. Clement Stone said, "Don't expect what you don't inspect."[15] That doesn't mean that you hover over every person involved and micromanage the process. Not at all.

But all of us need accountability. If you are embarking on a new life journey as an executive or as an entrepreneur, one of the greatest things you could do is find a couple of "strategic partners" who will encourage you and affirm you along the way, but who also will hold you accountable for the results to which you have committed.

When I committed to writing this book, it would have never happened without the constant encouragement of a couple of strategic partners who are also coaching partners. But they also asked the tougher questions: Did you write today? How did the writing go this week? How are you coming with this section of the book?

As an example, at one point I was standing in a grocery store getting ready to go through the checkout line when one of my strategic partners called me just to see how the writing was going. She was on a road trip but thought it was time to check in. I'm glad she did for I hadn't yet written that day—and wouldn't. But I made sure to schedule an extended writing session for the next day.

Why? Because one of my partners would be calling soon. And I'm glad they did. That's how projects get finished; it's how goals get accomplished. It's how this book was written.

If you're leading your organization with a new plan, undoubtedly it has gotten translated and communicated down to every division, every department, and every office. Every person has committed to certain initiatives or behaviors and goals—even you as the leader.

The plan that you helped your company put in place serves as an accountability tool for you the leader as well. Make sure those who report to you understand this. It helps those you lead to know that you, too, have skin in the game as well. You're not just the hotshot CEO sitting in his corner office in the ivory tower, giving the orders and directives. You're traveling with them. You're also working hard to reach the destination. Wait—you're actually leading them. That will make a difference.

Use Your Plan as a Measuring Stick

Closely akin to accountability but somewhat different, using your plan as a measuring stick is crucial to reaching your destination or achieving your goals.

If done right, your plan did not just focus on the end result but included strategies and tasks that were important to the accomplishment of those goals. The plan then serves as a wonderful measuring stick to answer the question, "Are we making progress?"

Perhaps an example will help. You're the marketing and sales director for a small start-up company. You've set an ambitious goal of doubling your sales revenue. That's a worthy goal and it will go a long way toward establishing your new company on a solid financial footing.

So your goal is to double your sales revenue by a certain date next year. What's your plan to do that? We all know that you increase revenue by making and closing more sales calls. But stop right there: That's not an adequate plan. It does not adequately address the true process that's involved in reaching your goal.

Let's try it again. Get real specific this time.

I want to double my sales revenue by a certain date next year. So . . .

- I will make 100 prospecting calls every week.

- I will contact five current customers every week to inquire how we can better serve them with the intent of increasing our business with them.

- I will update and create new marketing materials and then revise them every quarter.

- I will attend at least one networking event every week.

- I will book our participation in one major trade show every other month.

Your original goal was to double your sales revenue by a specific time next year. I'm suggesting you don't even focus on that. It's like sitting on your patio and shouting at your lawn, "Grow!"

Doubling your sales revenue is a byproduct—a byproduct of the process. Focus instead on the process, which is represented by the five activities you've committed to in your plan.

And, by focusing on those, they not only become a way for your boss or strategic partner to hold you accountable, they become a measuring stick.

At the end of the week, the accountability questions become very easy. How many prospecting calls did I make this week? How many current customers did I connect with this week? What steps have I taken to upgrade our marketing materials? Did I attend a networking event this week? How many major trade shows have we participated in? Are we on target for our participation in the next one?

Yes? No? If no, what happened? If no, what steps can you take this week to improve your weekly score and guarantee the overall goal being achieved.

Now translate that to your organization. What daily and/or weekly process goals do your people have in place? It might be in the area of sales or expense reduction. Maybe you've initiated a process to massively improve your customer service or deliver your product or service in a quicker fashion.

Your plan has become an accountability tool and a measuring stick. Both will help you and your organization reach the chosen destination.

Focus on the Twenty Percent

My third and final suggestion promotes something that almost everyone knows about but, in my experience, very few practice. And, from discussions I've had with other executives and corporate leaders, it's not unique to me.

For years, like many executives, I gave lip service to the 80/20 principle but really didn't use it in my planning and execution of plans. It was a brilliant theoretical principle; I even taught it—more than once. But I didn't really practice it . . . until recently.

Undoubtedly, especially if you have studied economics, you are familiar with what has come to be known as the Pareto Principle. It gets its name from its creator, Vilfredo Federico Damaso Pareto, an Italian philosopher and economist born in 1848.

According to the Pareto legend, one day he noticed, "Twenty percent of the pea plants in his garden generated 80 percent of the healthy peapods."[16] This observation led Pareto to begin looking around at other realities, and he began to notice some definite patterns in his universe.

For example, he discovered that 80 percent of the land in Italy was owned by 20 percent of the population. Looking at numerous industries he observed that 80 percent of production came from just 20 percent of the companies.

Everywhere he turned, the same pattern revealed itself. His hypothesis was borne out from his empirical research, and thus the Pareto Principle came to be.

Eighty percent of results will come from just twenty percent of the action.

–Pareto Principle

Pareto's principle has come to be known as the 80/20 rule. It's important to point out that it's not a rule in that all the figures always add up to exactly 80 and 20 percent. However, the principle can be seen throughout numerous business scenarios.

- Twenty percent of your sales reps will produce 80 percent of your total sales.

- Twenty percent of your customers will account for 80 percent of your total profits.

- Twenty percent of your clients will provide 80 percent of your customer service issues.

- Twenty percent of your new initiatives will produce 80 percent of your new growth.

New York Times best-selling author Kevin Kruse has pointed out that the 80/20 principle applies to his personal life as well. For example, he owns five suits but 80 percent of the time he grabs one in particular.

He has fifteen rooms in his house but he spends 80 percent of his time in 20 percent of the rooms. When he goes grocery shopping, he spends most his time in the "aisles that are around the edges of the store . . . and generally skips the aisles in the middle of the store." On his smartphone, he has 48 different apps. But 80 percent of his time is spent with the same eight that are on his home screen.

While his personal survey is interesting, perhaps his most important conclusion comes from his formal time management research. In an article, he stated:

> In my research into the productivity habits of high achievers, I interviewed hundreds of self-made millionaires, straight-A students and even Olympic athletes. For them, handling every task that gets thrown their way—or even every task that they would like to handle—is impossible. They use Pareto to help them determine what is of vital importance. Then, they delegate the rest, or simply let it go.[17]

A ONE-ON-ONE COACHING SESSION WITH DAVE

So how do you apply this principle to the plan you're creating for yourself or your organization? Let's ask some questions to help you apply the principle.

- What will be the best use of your limited resources?

- What is the best use of your team's limited time?

- What are the most important goals that are coming out of your planning process?

- What are the most important tasks that will contribute the most toward achieving the priority goals?

- Who are the clients that provide you the greatest revenue?

- What do you or your organization do that yields the greatest results?

We could ask questions like this all day long, but here's the point: As you create your plan, focus your time, money, energy, attention, your team's focus and effort, your goals, plans, and your blood, sweat, and tears on the 20 percent that will produce 80 percent of the results you're after.

And forget about the rest.

For a detailed list of resources to help you apply the Pareto Principle to your situation, go to IntentionalLeadershiptheBook.com/Pareto.

4

WHAT'S THE FINISH LINE?

However beautiful the strategy, you should occasionally look at the results.

—Sir Winston Churchill

Let's spend a few minutes talking again about your destination. You do want to get there, right? You're really heading toward a goal, aren't you? Then sooner or later, you need to think about the endgame.

Several questions rise to the surface. When will you get there? How long do you think this journey is going to take? What will be the indicators that you have arrived at your destination? Put another way, how will you know when you get there? What will happen when you get there?

Here's why these questions are so important.

THE IMPORTANCE OF A FINISH LINE

Endless journeys produce endless frustration. Nothing is more defeating or discouraging than to work and strive and reach, only to realize you know little about whether or not you're making any progress or if you're any closer to your goal.

Recall when you took your young children on that vacation road trip, and the endless questions—"Are we there yet?" "How much longer?" "When are we going to get there?"

Children become adults (usually). But even as adults, unbelievable frustration builds when we travel toward something without any idea of when the trip will end.

This journey you're taking your company on must have a definite destination and finish line. You must have a stopping point—a point of arrival—where people can celebrate the progress and accomplishment. There must be a time to exhale and relax for a few moments.

That's why the work you've done up until this point is so important. Having a definite destination is vital. Putting a mark on the wall and being able to say, "That's where we are going," makes a far larger difference than you can imagine.

As we've already stated, knowing the *why* will serve as a constant reminder, especially during the long days of work and striving. Remember, it's during the journey (process) that adversity shows up and obstacles arise. The *why* will help you and your people overcome them.

The plan that you have worked so hard on has become a measuring stick that will show your organization how far you've already come on this incredibly important journey. And progress is important.

Progress lifts morale. Again, think back. Wasn't it just a little helpful to be able to tell your kids you were halfway there? That it would only be two more hours? Or for them to know (if they were a little older) that you had already gone 400 miles and had only 150 more miles to go? Of course it was.

That's because progress lifts morale at any age. Having a finish line is crucial. Knowing that you're getting closer is even more important. It helps keep your eye on the goal. The more we take our eyes off the goal—the more we look away from our ultimate destination—the greater the odds grow that we'll miss it.

Progress lifts morale at any age.

Keeping the destination clear and at the forefront of your consciousness or in the minds of those in your organization greatly increases the odds that you'll get there. One of your jobs as the leader of the organization is to continually refine the focus. Another job is to communicate the progress you're making. More about that next.

Another consideration for me personally is that during a long journey, I can get bored. My mind will wander, I'll get distracted and even lose focus at times or suffer from vision leak. I keep my important, laminated documents in a prominent place on my desk to remind me where I'm headed, why I'm going there, the plan I'm following—and how I will know that I have arrived.

HOW WILL YOU KNOW WHEN YOU GET THERE?

Have you ever had the experience of arriving at your chosen destination without knowing you were there? Or am I the only oddball who's experienced that absurdity?

As preposterous as it may sound, you need to know when you've arrived at your destination. Even more important is to be able to know where you are at all times along the way.

That's why you include metrics and measurements in your system, to show you where you're making progress and where growth is lacking.

Earlier I talked about knowing where you are when you start. The point was if you don't know where you are at the beginning, you won't know how to get where you want to go.

Knowing the destination, however, is also a vital piece of information to have at your fingertips. Your metrics and measurements will not only show you where you are going, they will tell you where you are on the journey, inform you of corrections you need to make along the way, and inspire you to consistently keep at it as you are edging closer and closer to your goal.

Let's take a look at the ingredients of a plan for recognizing the destination.

Metrics and Measurements

One of the ways to know when you get there is to take a look at the metrics and measurements you put in place through your plan to judge progress.

Using the scenario mentioned in the last chapter, let's say you've set a goal and put a plan in place to grow your company's annual gross revenue by 100 percent over the next three years. Your organization's current annual income is $3 million. In three years, you want it to be $6 million.

Doubling your revenue is your clear destination—that's your *where*. You've come to grips with the *why* question and, along with your best people, have put together a plan to achieve it. In detail, you wanted to increase your revenue by 25 percent the first year, 35 percent the second year, and then a whopping 40 percent the third year.

So you have your targets set. Your best predictions tell you that if everything goes as planned, at the end of your first year your company's revenue will be at $3.75 million.

As you continue on your journey, if you're on track, your second year's revenue will rise to $4.8 million. And finally, by the end of year three, your company will reach your destination goal of $6 million. Undoubtedly, you will break those numerical targets down even further into quarterly goals as well.

Your progress is determined by whether or not you're meeting your quarterly and annual metrics along the way. What you'll discover is that marking those milestones will contribute to the rising morale that comes with your progress. If you're on target, a few small pauses to celebrate are more than warranted and will increase morale even more.

Midcourse Corrections Seal the Deal

But let's say you're not on target. For some reason, you are lagging behind and you've missed a few milestones. Don't panic or rush in and make massive changes.

There's a good chance some tweaks are in order. In fact, that will be a must. It is the midcourse corrections you will make (and probably more than once) that will help ensure you remain on course to meet the rest of your milestones and objectives, and reach your ultimate goal.

Life is all about making corrections along the way. This is certainly true on a personal level. How are you doing with your plan to get your finances in order and get out of debt? Or, you're on a mission to lose 50 pounds—are you making progress? Are you on target or are you lagging behind?

Or, the destination that was this book—I had a deadline with my publisher; the initial draft for this book needed to be finished by a certain date and the draft needed to be written with a word count target. So to meet my publisher's goal, I needed to write "x" number of words each day to beat my deadline.

If I am lagging behind in my debt payoffs, I need to tweak my process. If you notice that your weight loss has reached a plateau, you will make some changes to kick your progress back into gear.

If my manuscript was short of my word count target, I have to pick up the pace or I will miss my destination.

When you fly, from the moment your flight takes off, weather and atmospheric conditions will cause your plane's navigation system to recalibrate its flight path—again and again and again. When you fly from San Francisco to Washington, DC, your plane will get rerouted countless times.

Pilots operate by what is called the "1-in-60" rule. The rule holds that if you are off course by just one degree at the start of your trip, after 60 minutes you'll be off course by one mile.

Over the course of time, one degree off course makes a remarkable difference. On that very same San Francisco to Washington, DC, flight, if no course alterations are made along the way, you'll land on the other side of Baltimore. You'll have missed your target by 42.6 miles.

That reality is just as true in your business. One consultant put it this way: "This is why you can't run your business on autopilot. If you don't set the course correctly in the beginning (which no one does—close, maybe, but not exactly), the odds of success are slim, at best. You've got to watch the results you're getting and make constant course corrections."

Always Communicate Where You Are

So let's say that at certain strategic points on the journey, you're not where you want to be, or where you planned to be. Often the question arises, "How much do I reveal about where we are?"

That depends on many, many issues. I am not an attorney and am not qualified to give legal advice. However, if you're a publicly traded company, you have a legal obligation to reveal everything regarding where you are in all of your financial matters.

If you have a board of directors, you probably have a legal obligation, if not a moral imperative, to share with your board where you are lagging behind in your initiatives and journey.

But—and this is my opinion—if none of the above conditions apply, you still have an ethical obligation to let your organization know where you are. Please note, I suggest this as a point of reference from experiences with both telling the whole story and holding back because I wanted to shield my people from discouraging news. Trust me—full disclosure is always the best policy.

Part of leadership is instilling confidence as well as garnering people's trust. How can you accomplish either of those objectives if you are neither transparent nor up front in your communication?

Progress is a morale booster. Lack of progress is not necessarily a morale killer. As your team journeys together, there will always be some reasonable and logical explanations for why you have missed some mile markers along the way. And, no doubt, the conclusion of your organization's players will be, "Okay, we didn't plan on that. But this is fixable. We can still make it."

Midcourse corrections help you get to where you're going, and problems are best solved at the lowest possible level. It might just be that when you communicate to your organization what areas are lagging behind, that might be all the encouragement one of your key people needs to come forward to say, "I've been watching this for a while." Or, "I've been thinking about this for a couple of weeks or months." "What if we tried this? What if we made this adjustment in our process? Would that make a difference?"

That person may have just the answer you are looking for. But she would have never made the suggestion if she thought everything was going smoothly.

One of your critical skills as a leader is your ability to communicate. So communicate—even if the message is not perfectly positive and glowing.

Obviously, give care and time to prepare how you want to communicate less than stellar news. Words matter. Tone matters. Context makes a difference. There will be a variety of ways to communicate what needs to be reported. Carefully choose the right one and trust your people to handle what needs to be done.

But communicate. Your people will thank you in the long run.

Here's why I believe this is so important.

Reality Is Your Friend

One of my mentors (from a distance), and indeed, one of my favorite people in the world, as you might have guessed, is Dr. Henry Cloud. More than one of his books are on what I call my "Life-Change Bookshelf." That means if there is ever a fire in my house, the first thing I do is grab the books on the "Life-Change Bookshelf." And then I look for my family members.

Dr. Cloud just makes sense to me.

In his book *Integrity*, he talks about possessing and operating with an "orientation toward truth."[18] Our purpose here is not to launch into a lengthy diatribe about character and ethics, but rather to point out that clearly letting your team know where your organization is on its journey to your desired destination is preferable over shielding them from difficult news.

This is precisely Cloud's point when he writes, "Truthfulness is really measured in terms of our tendency to tell it when it *hurts* in some way. People fudge or lie when there is a risk of some sort of loss or negative consequence."

He continues, "The tendency to hide the truth where there are potential consequences is a part of human nature, and sadly, one that usually makes us incur more negative consequences than if we had told the truth."

The logical and, I believe, correct conclusion is that "the consequences of deceit are usually greater than the consequences of truth."

At a strategic place in Dr. Cloud's book is the callout:

Reality is always your friend.

In my copy, there is a box around it and exclamation points next to it, and I have written the words: "ALWAYS REMEMBER THIS!!!" You can't know how many times I have had to repeat that to myself when I've discovered bad news or been informed of less than perfect results.

Sadly, I would like to ignore it. And in earlier, more immature years I would have and did. But not now. I have learned the hard way that reality, no matter how difficult or complicated it might be, really is my friend. And everything else is a fantasy.

Reality is always your friend and it can serve as the trigger to help you pull together and do whatever is necessary to reach your chosen destination.

In his book *Good to Great*, Jim Collins echoes this important principle. His research has shown that one of the characteristics of good-to-great companies is their undying willingness to "confront the brutal facts."

I love his assertion: "There is nothing wrong with pursuing a vision for greatness. After all, the good-to-great companies also set out to create greatness. But unlike the comparison companies [those that fell short of the good-to-great characteristics], the good-to-great companies continually refined the *path* to greatness with the brutal facts of reality."

After all, as Winston Churchill pointed out, "There is no worse mistake in public leadership than to hold out false hopes soon to be swept away."

Dr. Cloud's conclusion, I think, is very instructive: "For us to get real results in the real world, we must be in touch with what is, not what we wish things were or think things should be or are led by others to believe they are. The only thing that is going to be real in the end is what is. That is where profits are going to be made . . ."

UPON ARRIVAL

So . . . you've gotten through some of the difficult moments just described. You've tweaked your processes and made some midcourse corrections, and all the metrics and measurements are indicating that you've met your goals. You've crossed your finish line.

Congratulations! What do you do now?

You acknowledge your success, and you communicate it to your team. As with the four questions you are answering in this process, communication is one of the ultimate demonstrations of your leadership—a reaffirmation of the culture you are creating within your organization or within your own life, to improve and grow. Part of the communication is a celebration.

5

CELEBRATING THE SUCCESS

The celebration of success overshadows the challenges that were encountered along the way.

—Jeffrey Benjamin

You did it. You've arrived at your destination. The long journey that began with asking the question, "Where are we going to go?" has been realized.

With your destination firmly embedded in your heart and mind, and a workable plan driving you along the way, you've just crossed the finish line. How do you know that you're there? All the metrics and measurements indicate that you have arrived. Your goals have been reached. You made it to your destination.

What now? Three things. They may seem obvious but too often they are overlooked. Make sure you don't overlook them.

CELEBRATE

It's time for a party . . . and not just any party. It's time to throw the biggest, baddest, most glorious and expensive bash you possibly can.

Seems superfluous, you think? Think again. Your people have worked hard—for quite a long time. They bought into the vision and direction. They signed on to go where you suggested the company should go.

They internalized the answer to the *why*. You may have suggested it, but they owned it. The organization's *why* became their *why*, and they adjusted motives and purposes along the way so that they could become part of something that was worth the effort.

They helped you formulate a workable plan to get there. And they executed the plan consistently and, most of the time, flawlessly. They worked hard—in fact, they probably put more effort toward the goal on their own time than you will ever know. That always happens when people catch the vision and the motivation.

And, now they've accomplished your goal. There had better be a party—and it needs to be a big one.

People always remember parties. Most of the time they will forget the hard work. They'll forget how difficult it was to figure out the solution to that plaguing problem that kept tripping up their department.

They'll forget the moments in the middle of the night when they woke up thinking about the problems they were facing in their office. They'll forget the seemingly endless meetings held to tweak the processes to get the results just right.

They'll even forget the frustration. But they will never forget the party. How can I be so sure? Because I still remember all the parties.

The parties to celebrate successful fundraising campaigns. The parties to commemorate record company growth. The celebrations to mark the completion of an intense three-year goal. The parties to celebrate just the fact that we did what we set out to do.

Earlier I referred to my malady of sometimes being joy challenged. Planning and executing completion celebrations have helped me get over that issue. These days, even while finalizing the destination and formulating the *why* and putting together the plan . . . I'm already thinking about the party.

So when your measures and feedback show you've accomplished your goals—arrived at your destination—take the time to let it sink in. Record it and communicate the success to your team.

And, let everyone know it's time to party, so they will remember it, too.

SHARE THE GLORY

One of the immutable laws[19] of my company is, "Teams win championships."

It might seem almost a little cheesy to say that, except that phrase is pregnant with meaning for my business partner and me. It's an ever-present reminder that accomplishing anything of significance is rarely done by one person.

History overflows with examples of incredibly talented people—sports stars, celebrities, entrepreneurs, inventors, scientists, business executives—who never accomplished much of anything until they brought a team alongside them.

There are unending platitudes and mottos that speak of the team's importance. Make them more than platitudes—make them a major part of your philosophical modus operandi.

That means when you have your party to celebrate your accomplishment, you have one job and one job only: share all the glory you can with all the people you can for as long as you can. Because, even though you're the leader, they deserve it far more than you do.

Let me give you a hint: they already know this truth, but it's good for them to know that you know it, too.

Celebration parties provide the perfect opportunity for you to publicly acknowledge key team members, players who went above the call of duty, staff members who consistently showed up, and those who did thankless tasks and excelled at seemingly menial roles.

This is the perfect opportunity for you to acknowledge people for just being who they are—people who are valuable and integral to the success of the entire organization.

I read an interesting article recently that illustrates this concept beautifully.[20] It was written by Mike Reiss, a writer for ESPN, who had the assignment of covering the National Football League team, the New England Patriots.

At the time of this writing, the Patriots have just won their fifth Super Bowl championship. New reports seemingly love to point out how they are the team that everybody loves—or hates. That sentiment extends to their record-setting coach, Bill Belichick. No matter what you might think of him, for the casual student of professional football, there is no denying he has created an unbelievable culture of winning and excellence.

Nowhere is that more obvious than in the concept of team that has been instilled within the organization. Reiss listed the top ten things he, as a reporter, learned about team building from covering the Patriots in general and, specifically, from watching Bill Belichick lead the team.

Number two on the list was, the "power of the team." According to Reiss, "One of the messages that players see on the door as they enter Gillette Stadium is to 'put the team first.'" That philosophy is portrayed every day by how business is conducted around the organization.

Nowhere was it more brilliantly seen than before Super Bowl XXXVI when the Patriots played the then-St. Louis Rams. Prior to that moment, at every Super Bowl when the teams were introduced, either the offensive unit or the defensive unit was introduced. In fact, the NFL insisted it be done that way.

Not this year, however. Though it had never been done before, and despite the NFL's insistence to the contrary, the

Patriots, led by Bill Belichick, said, "No, we are a team—that's the way we will be introduced."

In other words, no one person or group was more important than the other. They were one unit. "The Patriots sent a message with their bold gesture, showing that it takes more than just talent to win on the game's biggest stage."

Reiss correctly points out that "getting a team to come together is one of the great challenges for any coach." It will be your greatest challenge as the leader in your organization as well.

So when you come together to party, don't just celebrate your accomplishment, celebrate your team, your people—each one of them. It's well worth the effort.

Find more resources detailing the Bill Belichick and New England Patriots philosophy of leadership and teamwork at IntentionalLeadershiptheBook.com/Patriots.

ASK THE QUESTION: "WHAT'S NEXT?"

I want to be very careful here because this can be easily misinterpreted.

Don't diminish or even cut short the celebration. Let the party prevail; but this is probably the perfect time to start broaching the subject on at least a casual basis and begin asking the question, "What's next?"

There are a couple of reasons why I toss this into the mix.

First, morale is extremely high at this point. Look at what you've accomplished. To continue with the revenue goal example, you've just doubled your annual gross revenue in only three years. It's the reason you're celebrating.

Your organization is already pondering, "I wonder what we could really do?" It's time to start thinking about stretching a little more and chatting with a few key people about the future.

- Where do you think we should go next?

- What's the next major goal for our company?

- Do you want to hear what I'm thinking about now?

Second, please remember, you're on an even bigger journey—as an individual or as an organization. Fitness coach Eric Stevens says, "Reaching the goal is a temporary mark and a means to an end. Setting the goal and hitting the goal is actually the starting place, not the destination."[21]

Whether you're leading yourself in a new initiative or leading your organization, the overall purpose for both of you is to continually move forward. Let's not forget the *why* that drove your initial endeavors in the first place—that *why* is probably still relevant.

"As a coach," Stevens says, "I've actually seen people get depressed after achieving and reaching a goal." Your goal as a leader at this point is celebration, not letdown.

Letdown does not have to be inevitable. As Stevens points out, "Our job is then to keep moving forward with a different perspective and continuing to establish the why."

So . . . it's never too soon to start asking the "What's next?" questions. This question will help you begin to sow some seeds for your next destination.

But remember to always link your new destination to your *why*. That's what connects where you just went with where you want to go next.

Now is the time to start. After all, what better moment than now to start thinking about the next party?

For a bonus list of goal-setting resources, go to
IntentionalLeadershiptheBook.com/goals.

6

THE FOUR-QUESTION
BUSINESS PLAN

*In preparing for battle, I have always found that
plans are useless but planning is indispensable.*

—Dwight D. Eisenhower

MY OPINION ON TRADITIONAL
BUSINESS PLANS

I'm not a big fan of business plans. There—I said it. I have
never liked them. Not a fan—at all. Here's why.

First, untold numbers of man-hours are spent putting them
together. Days are spent sequestered in a room somewhere
postulating and speculating about who your ideal customer is,
formulating the catchiest mission statement and/or vision statement, and crystalizing your values.

When you're done, it's printed up in a spiffy presentation binder and handed out to all those you believe should read it. After sitting in their inbox for a day or two or week or three, it might get looked at before it is placed on my shelf to gather dust along with my master's thesis that was written 30 years ago.

A bank *might* look at it—maybe. A venture capitalist will not. He or she is too busy to spend any time with your document.

Second, all those untold numbers of man-hours cost money. Most often the team putting together the business plan is taken from the personnel that are at the highest levels of the company, thus earning the most money.

If we multiply the number of hours spent on the plan by the amount of income that our high-level team members earn, we'll discover that the ROI for this project doesn't make sense at any level.

Third, a business plan is speculation and conjecture at best, and a total shot in the dark at worst. The best guess confidently states that our plan will not even come close to being realized.

Alexander Osterwalder has correctly asserted, "Founders go wrong when they start to believe their business plan will materialize as written. I advise entrepreneurs to burn their business plan—it's simply too dangerous to the health of your business."

Whoa! I am not suggesting that you burn your business plan. But I am proposing that you take a look at what makes up your plan.

In the old days, business plans were anywhere from 75 to 100 pages in length. Okay, if yours is that long, yes, go ahead and burn it. That's ludicrous. Some have suggested that it should be more like ten to fifteen pages. Again, too long—burn it.

This reality is what has made "the lean startup method" so popular today. The phenomenon began as an idea and developed into a method. But it has exploded into a movement, made even more popular by Eric Ries' book *The Lean Startup*.[22]

Ries suggests that one of the reasons start-ups fail at such a rapid rate is what he calls "the allure of a good plan." Harking back to an earlier era, things like "a solid strategy and thorough market research" could be and were often indicators of likely success.

"The overwhelming temptation," he says, "is to apply them to start-ups, too, but this doesn't work, because startups operate with too much uncertainty. Start-ups do not yet know who their customer is or what their product should be. As the world becomes more uncertain, it gets harder and harder to predict the future."

"But I'm not leading a start-up," you respond. Indeed you may not be. Keep in mind, however, that at least some of the readers of this book will be. More importantly, I'll repeat one of Ries' statements because it applies to all organizations and individuals:

As the world becomes more uncertain, it gets harder and harder to predict the future.

–Eric Ries

There are two things I know for sure: 1) our world is changing at a rate faster than at any time in our history, and 2) the rate of change is only going to increase.

That's why Osterwalder suggests that you and I burn our business plans. Intriguing as that might be, let me present an alternative to lighting a match.

While the traditional business plan is outdated, unnecessary, and a waste of time—and while even a ten- to fifteen-page business plan is not worth your time and energy, what about a simple, straightforward, easy-to-understand and remember, one-page business plan?

I read many articles advocating this new approach. Make it short and simple. Like the product or service you're introducing—get it to market quickly. Make the necessary changes and improvements in future iterations.

You can find all kinds of models, instruction sheets, templates, and suggestions for creating your one-page business plan almost anywhere you look. But here's my proposal.

THE FOUR-QUESTION BUSINESS PLAN

If you follow the outline that I have presented here, you've already done the work—you have the basics of your one-page business plan. Many will suggest you put all kinds of things into your plan, even though it is only one page. You'll read phrases like mission statement, BHAGS, budget, annual income projection, value proposition, customer segments, key resources, key activities, key partnerships, and revenue streams. Even as I write this paragraph, I'm reaching for a match.

I'm suggesting that your one-page business plan simply answer the four questions featured in this book:

1. Where are you going?

What are you trying to accomplish? What are you going to do? Where are you, either as an individual making a major life change, or a company trying to take new territory, trying to go?

2. Why are you going there?

Remember what Simon Sinek said. "People don't buy *what* you do, they buy *why* you do it." *Why* relates to your mission—your purpose. That's why you don't need to devote time and precious space to a mission or vision statement. Your *why* will answer those questions.

3. How will you get there?

In other words—"What's the plan?" What are the strategies you will employ? How will those strategies play out in terms of tactics? Who is responsible for what? What department owns this segment? Who will lead the way with that initiative?

This will perhaps be the longest section of your plan but it will still not need to take up that much space.

4. How will you know when you get there?

Again—"What's the destination?" What are the results you're after? What are the milestones and time-frames? What are the indicators that you are making progress or that you have reached your goals?

Just four simple questions and four simple answers. Everything can fit neatly on one page.

Visit IntentialLeadershiptheBook.com/plan for a downloadable template.

WHY THIS FORMAT WORKS

I've used this tool in leading organizations of all sizes. I've started or helped start three companies over the last seven years. I've used the one-page business plan in each one. And, I used it long before I ever read anyone who suggested it.

Here's why I think it's so effective—it's short. That's it—it's short. But its length, or lack of it, brings with it at least four benefits that cannot be ignored.

First, because it's short, it will get read. To continue with the example that has wound its way throughout the book, you want to double your annual gross revenue in three years. So you bring in a new Chief Technology Officer (CTO). He's sitting at his desk the first day on the job, perusing all the HR materials—forms to be completed, policy manuals, etc. There is an orientation packet that includes the one-page business plan that is your road map for the next three years.

If it's any longer than one page, it will probably get shoved to the side for a couple of days, or worse, get slipped into his briefcase to be read somewhere down the road (which is a euphemism for never). You want to make sure it gets read.

You're having lunch with a potential investor in your company. If you hand her a 50-page plan, it will probably never get read, or at best, will be summarized by some junior staffer in the next couple of months. Hand her a one-page plan, she'll probably quickly read it at the table enabling more in-depth discussion about what you're trying to do and how she can become part of it.

Second, because it's short, your plan is more easily remembered. That means its contents are more easily referenced—at lunch meetings, over coffee, in staff meetings, at the water cooler, even in the elevator to and from the parking garage.

A short business plan becomes a declaration—

This is where we're going. This is why we're going there. And, by the way, this is how we're going to get there. And when we're done, this is what we'll have accomplished.

Easily remembered means more easily executed—which is what you're after.

Third, because it's short, your plan is more easily reviewable. Earlier I mentioned the laminated documents I review regularly—every couple of weeks, if not weekly. My one-page business plan is among those documents. A 75-page business plan wouldn't even go in the file. And it definitely wouldn't go in my briefcase on a flight to Los Angeles or Chicago.

A one-page business plan gets slipped in with other important documents. Why? Because I'll want to review it before key meetings and appointments. A short document aids in that preparation process.

Finally, because it's short, your plan is easily revised and adjusted. Forget editing a 75-page business plan and reprinting it for everyone. That won't happen.

It is much easier, however, to adjust a one-page plan and give a revised copy to all your team members. Remember, one of the keys mentioned earlier is the midcourse corrections that will be made in your plan to help you reach your destination.

So, back to our example—you're halfway through year two of your journey. The second quarter numbers come in and you realize that a couple of tweaks need to be made in your strategy to get to your second-year goal of a 35-percent increase in your annual gross revenue.

Your team has met and come up with some new tactics or a revised sales strategy. How easy is it to plug these changes into a one-page document and give every person a revised game plan for achieving your goals? It's literally that simple.

So here's my challenge and encouragement to you. Whether you're launching on your own in a brand-new direction or wanting to take your organization to the next level, definitely have a plan.

A plan is important because it brings clarity, and clarity is the path to profit and success. But keep it short and simple.

- Where are we going?
- Why are we going there?
- How will we get there?
- How will we know when we get there?

Finally . . . relax and enjoy the ride.

CONCLUSION

While one should never assume, if you're reading this page, I'm assuming you have stuck with me throughout the book.

If that's the case, a heartfelt "thank you" is in order. I appreciate your interest and commitment to learning about intentional leadership and becoming a better, more intentional leader.

I love leadership. I love talking about it, studying it, teaching it, developing it, coaching it, doing it, and now, writing about it. I don't know where it came from but it certainly resides in my DNA.

What I love most about leadership is getting better at it.

One of my coaching partners recently took us through a personal development module focused on being more proactive about one's future. An assignment given to us was to come up with what she called a "prioritized list of operationalized core values."

No surprise—"growth" made my list. I like to get better. We all do.

A mentor of mine, for most of my leadership career, said it best.

Everyone wins when a leader gets better.

—Bill Hybels

Because we don't live on a deserted island, that reality possesses ramifications for all of us. If you're reading this book, chances are you operate in some type of leadership capacity. You might be an entrepreneur, company CEO or COO, teacher, coach, division head, department chairman, or team leader. If you're a parent, you're leading your family.

No matter what group you fall into, the reality for you is everyone wins when you get better.

That's one of the reasons my business partner and I started The New Harbor Company (NewHarborCo.com). We want to help leaders, executives, and organizations get better. Writing this book was part of that endeavor.

So, my final piece of coaching advice to you is this: GO FOR IT! Become more intentional in your leadership. Ask the questions; figure out the *where*, the *why*, and the *how*. Celebrate the success of crossing the finish line.

And then watch the ripple effect—in your company and your community. Because everybody wins when you get better.

ACKNOWLEDGMENTS

One of the immutable laws of my company states, "Teams win championships." It serves as a reminder that not much of anything significant is achieved individually. It always requires others—a team.

Writing and publishing a book is certainly no different. This book was birthed by a team and I am deeply grateful and humbly indebted to everyone who played a crucial role.

Maryanna Young, CEO of Aloha Publishing, has been a long-time dear friend and for more than a decade prodded me to write something. Maryanna, thank you for your friendship and persistent encouragement. It finally paid off.

Laura Cesare and Jen Regner, two members of Aloha's editorial team, waded through my initial thoughts and words and expertly organized them to make sense. Their competent and kind shepherding helped make this book a reality.

Amy Hoppock, one of my coaching partners and the "Queen of Maximizers," helped shape the final product. Amy, your friendship, humor, unending encouragement, and profound thinking has helped sharpen my own thought process and made my message clearer and more succinct.

To my best friend, college sweetheart, and wife of almost 40 years, Kathy: I owe you everything. You once told me I was "born to write." I don't know if that's true, but without your influence, no one would be reading these words. Thank you.

Finally, to you the reader . . . thank you. Thank you for picking up this book, for trusting me, for reading, and for joining me on the journey of intentional leadership. I hope you enjoy the ride.

ABOUT THE AUTHOR

Dave Weitz is a leader of people and organizations, as well as a dynamic communicator. He has impacted thousands of lives with his communication and leadership skills. His passion is bringing out greatness in the people he leads and serves. He has a unique ability to communicate vision, purpose, and meaning—and out of that rare and special gift has come growth of the people he leads and the organizations he guides.

Dave's primary laboratory for learning and development of his communication skills and ability to solve complex personnel problems, manage multimillion dollar budgets and projects, work with a board of directors, and develop other leaders came as a pastor. For over 25 years, Dave led churches, large and small, and in each one served as a dynamic and effective leader.

A deep understanding of leadership and the ability to communicate clearly led Dave naturally, while still a pastor, to become a leadership coach and consultant to the CEOs and executives he knew, as well as their companies. He also served as a corporate trainer, providing quarterly leadership development for franchise owners and managers of an international corporation during his pastoral years.

Groups of people working toward a common purpose can easily become messy with personal disputes, misunderstandings, dishonesty, and a plethora of other minefields that create division. Dave has led teams, churches, and other leaders through adversity and challenge. He looks to approach challenging situations with a goal of restoring unity and finding common ground. He is able to apply the lessons he has learned to help his clients navigate their own challenging situations.

As a coach and consultant, Dave has leveraged all of his pastoral, business consulting, and communication skills to invest intentionally and with great wisdom in the clients he serves. As a life-long learner and voracious reader, he has been able to apply his personal experiences and his vast exposure to great thinkers, practitioners, and authors to create personalized insights for each of his clients. Dave is passionate about helping his clients reach the next level in their professional and personal life.

Dave cofounded The New Harbor Company with his son and business partner, Adam. Their mission is not complicated: We help executives, leaders and organizations get better. Find out more about the company and its work at NewHarborCo.com.

Dave lives in Boise, Idaho, with his wife Kathy and their black Lab Beau. On his best days, you'll find him outside a local coffee shop with them, a good friend, or a great book. You might also find him somewhere on a Harley.

If you'd like Dave to speak at your next event or want to explore coaching or consulting with him, or if you want to find out what he's been thinking and reading, you can follow him at DaveWeitz.com.

NOTES

1. Trent Hamm, "Simple Doesn't Mean Easy," (www.TheSimpleDollar. com, June 23, 2016).

2. Robert E. Quinn, *Deep Change: Discovering the Leader Within* (San Francisco: Jossey-Bass Inc., Publishers, 1996).

3. Thomas J. Peters and Robert H. Waterman, Jr., *In Search of Excellence: Lessons from America's Best-Run Companies* (New York: HarperCollins Publishers, 1982).

4. Caitlin Johnson, "Cutting Through Advertising Clutter," September 17, 2006, http://www.cbsnews.com/news/cutting-through-advertising-clutter/.

5. Frederick Buechner, *Wishful Thinking: A Theological* ABC (New York: Harper & Row Publishers, 1973).

6. Simon Sinek, *Start with Why: How Great Leaders Inspire Everyone to Take Action* (New York: The Penguin Group, 2009).

7. John Battelle, "The Birth of Google" (*Wired Magazine*, August 1, 2005).

8. Bill Carmody, "Why 96 Percent of Businesses Fail Within 10 Years" (Inc. August 12, 2015).

9. You can read more about this wonderful cause in: Amy Hoppock, Dottie Bledsoe, Lauren Phillips and Maryanna Young, *Compelled by Love: The Story of Run 4 Heaven's Gate* (Eagle, Idaho: Aloha Publishing, 2015).

10. http://www.nasa.gov/missions/highlights/webcasts/shuttle/sts111/ shuttle_qa.html

11. BHAG stands for "Big Hairy Audacious Goal." It was made popular in Jim Collins's book, *Good to Great: Why Some Companies Make the Leap and Others Don't* (New York: HarperCollins Publishers, Inc., 2001).

12. Drew Hansen, "Mahalia Jackson, and King's Improvisation" (*The New York Times*, August 27, 2013).

13. Jim Collins, *Good to Great: Why Some Companies Make the Leap and Others Don't* (New York: HarperCollins Publishers, Inc., 2001).

14. Dr. Henry Cloud, *9 Things You Simply Must Do to Succeed in Love and Life* (Brentwood Tennessee: Integrity Publishers, 2004).

15. W. Clement Stone, *The Success System That Never Fails* (Wilder Publications, 2009). Originally published in 1962.

16. Kevin Kruse, "The Pareto Principle for Time Management." (www.kevinkruse.com, March 15, 2016).

17. Kevin Kruse, *15 Secrets Successful People Know About Time Management: The Productivity Habits of 7 Billionaires, 13 Olympic Athletes, 29 Straight-A Students, and 239 Entrepreneurs* (Philadelphia: The Kruse Group, 2015).

18. Dr. Henry Cloud, *Integrity: The Courage to Meet the Demands of Reality* (New York: HarperCollins Publishers, 2006).

19. "Immutable laws" is a phrase I picked up from Mike Michalowics in his book, *The Toilet Paper Entrepreneur* (Boonton, New Jersey: Obsidian Launch, LLC, 2008).

20. Mike Reiss, "What We've Learned from Covering Bill Belichick's Patriots Teams." (http://www.espn.com/blog/new-england-patriots/post/_/id/4793808/what-weve-learned-from-covering-bill-belichicks-patriots-teams, Jul9 9, 2016).

21. Eric C. Stevens, "And Then What? What Happens After We Reach Our Goals?" (https://breakingmuscle.com/sports-psychology/and-then-what-what-happens-after-we-reach-our-goals).

22. Eric Ries, *The Lean Startup: How Today's Entrepreneurs Use Continuous Innovation to Create Radically Successful Businesses* (New York: Crown Business, 2011).

YOUR NOTES

CPSIA information can be obtained
at www.ICGtesting.com
Printed in the USA
LVHW012019130622
721185LV00004B/403